CW00524035

JEMMA KENNEDY

Jemma Kennedy is a novelist, playwright and screenwriter.
After a career in the music business in London and New York,
she published her first novel, *Skywalking*, in 2003. Recent plays
include *The Prince and the Pauper* and *The Summer Book*
(Unicorn Theatre); *The Grand Irrationality* (Lost Theatre
Studio, Los Angeles); *Don't Feed the Animals* (National Theatre
Connections); *The Gift* (New Vic Theatre, Stoke-on-Trent) and
Second Person Narrative for Tonic Theatre's inaugural Platform
play series. Jemma was Pearson Playwright in Residence at the
National Theatre in 2010. She is currently writing her first stage
musical *Electric Ladies* for Universal Music. Films credits
include *Captain Webb* (Marathon Films) and recent screenplay
adaptations of Barbara Pym's novel *Excellent Women* for
Raindog/BBC Films and *Crooked Heart* by Lissa Evans for
Braven/BBC Films. Her book on playwriting will be published
soon by Nick Hern Books.

Other Titles in this Series

Jemma Kennedy

GENESIS INC.

NICK HERN BOOKS

London

www.nickhernbooks.co.uk

A Nick Hern Book

Genesis Inc. first published in Great Britain in 2018 as a paperback original by Nick Hern Books Limited, The Glasshouse, 49a Goldhawk Road, London W12 8QP

Genesis Inc. copyright © 2018 Jemma Kennedy
Music copyright © 2018 Jemma Kennedy and Zara Nunn

Jemma Kennedy has asserted her moral right to be identified as the author of this work

Cover image: SWD

Designed and typeset by Nick Hern Books, London
Printed in Great Britain by Mimeo Ltd, Huntingdon, Cambridgeshire PE29 6XX

A CIP catalogue record for this book is available from the British Library

ISBN 978 1 84842 768 6

Genesis Inc. was first performed at Hampstead Theatre, London, on 22 June 2018, with the following cast:

JEFF/ABRAHAM/ EMBRYOLOGIST	Oliver Alvin-Wilson
SERENA/SARAH	Ritu Arya
KIKI/NARRATOR/ SERENA'S OVARY/ DAISY/HAGAR/TEENAGER/ MEDIC	Kirsty Besterman
MILES/ABRAHAM/MEDIC	Arthur Darvill
DR MARSHALL/KARL MARX/ MESSENGER 1/GOD	Harry Enfield
BRIDGET/SERENA'S OVARY/ MESSENGER 2/MEDIC	Laura Howard
SERENA'S VAGINA/MITA/ SERVANT/GREAT GRANDMOTHER/MEDIC/ SURGEON/	Shobu Kapoor
LARISSA/SHARON/SERENA'S OVARY/MESSENGER 3/ NURSE/SUSAN SONTAG/ MEDIC	Clare Perkins
FATHER SCALES/ISHMAEL/ MORTGAGE ADVISER/ NURSE/MEDIC/SECURITY GUARD	Arthur Wilson

And Jenni Murray as THE VOICE OF THE WOMB

Director	Laurie Sansom
Designer	Jess Curtis
Lighting	Oliver Fenwick
Composition	Zara Nunn
Sound	Gareth Fry
Video	Ian William Galloway
Movement	Georgina Lamb
Casting	Suzanne Crowley and Gilly Poole

Acknowledgements

Thanks are due to the many people who helped me with the genesis, research and development of this play: Mita Banerjee, Nina Barnsley at Donor Conception Network, Professor Susan Bewley, Sebastian Born, Sandie Chhabra, Judy Counihan, Ryan Craig, Marianne Elliott, Amy Hodge, Jennifer Hunt, Dr Paul Kennedy, Dr Yacoub Khalaf, Miranda Kingsley, Dr Fiona Kisby, Dr James Monarch, Purni Morell, Natalie Gamble Associates, Sarah Norcross at Progress Educational Trust, Zara Nunn, John Parsons, Victoria Sadler, Natalie Singer, Giles Smart, Kate Thomson, Parisa Vakili, Professor Robert Winston, Miriam Zoll.

Thank you Ed Hall, Greg Ripley-Duggan and all at Hampstead Theatre.

Thank you Oliver Alvin-Wilson, Ritu Arya, Kirsty Besterman, Arthur Darvill, Harry Enfield, Laura Howard, Shobu Kapoor, Clare Perkins and Arthur Wilson.

Thank you Jenni Murray for being my womb.

Hugest thanks to Laurie Sansom, undefeatable disco midwife.

The following books provided useful resources and insight:

A Child Against All Odds by Robert Winston

Cracked Open by Miriam Zoll

What Money Can't Buy: The Moral Limits of Markets by Michael J. Sandel

The Baby Business by Debora L. Spar

J.K.

For Marcel

Characters

BRIDGET, *forty-two*
MILES, *forty*
JEFF, *thirties*
SERENA, *thirties*
DR MARSHALL, *fifties*
LARISSA, *fifties*
MITA, *sixties*
FATHER SCALES, *twenties*
DAISY, *thirties*
SHARON, *fifties*
KIKI
MORTGAGE ADVISER
EMBRYOLOGIST
NURSE
MALE NURSE
SECURITY GUARD

GOD
KARL MARX
ABRAHAM
SARAH
HAGAR
ISHMAEL
MESSENGERS 1, 2, 3
SERVANT
TEENAGER
SUSAN SONTAG
GREAT-GRANDMOTHER
VOICEOVERS: JENNI MURRAY, NARRATOR,
   SCHOOL TANNOY, OVARIES, VAGINA, WOMB

The play can be performed with a minimum of nine actors
Doubling as suggested:

Actor 1: Miles / Abraham
Actor 2: Bridget / Serena's Ovary 1 / Messenger 2
Actor 3: Serena / Sarah
Actor 4: Jeff / Abraham / Embryologist
Actor 5: Dr Marshall / Karl Marx / God / Messenger 1
Actor 6: Larissa / Sharon / Messenger 3 / Nurse / Susan Sontag
Actor 7: Mita / Serena's Vagina / Servant / Surgeon /
    Great-Grandmother
Actor 8: Kiki / Daisy / Serena's Ovary 2 / Hagar / Teenager
Actor 9: Father Scales / Mortgage Adviser / Security Guard /
    Male Nurse / Ishmael

*This text went to press before the end of rehearsals and so may
differ slightly from the play as performed.*

ACT ONE

Scene One

DR MARSHALL *onstage. He is a practised public speaker and
enjoys his performance tremendously.*

MARSHALL. I'll conclude, if I may, with a reminder that we
are doctors of fertility, not gods. And yet some days, when
I have to face yet another desperate patient, it feels that the
fate of future generations lies entirely in our hands. Take
'Yasmin'. Failed by the NHS, now separated from her
partner, and still battling her unexplained infertility. Or
'Jane', who wakes alone on the day after her fortieth birthday
in the flat she worked so hard to buy, parched with vodka and
regret, as the front door quietly shuts behind the second
cousin's married friend – and hears the shrill alarm of eternal
absence. What should I tell these women, and hundreds just
like them, when they come to me for help? That forgoing
motherhood is the price of Jane's career? That Yasmin's
failure to conceive is a tragedy without solution? What I tell
them is this. That they must have faith. In science. In our
industry. In *us*. (*A change of gear.*) Fellow doctors,
colleagues, peers. This is not the time for caution, but for
courage, innovation and investment. Only then can we lead
a reproductive revolution that will give our patients the
chance to go forth, be fruitful, and multiply, and fill the earth.

Scene Two

Same day. Genesis Inc. clinic waiting room. A reception desk.
A wall of baby photos, embryo scans and thank-you cards.

SERENA *and* JEFF *sit waiting.* SERENA *writes forms.*
JEFF *has a cycle helmet with him. We can hear the tail end of*
MARSHALL*'s speech on the waiting room radio.*

MARSHALL.…be fruitful and multiply, and fill the earth.

> *Applause on the radio, then the voice of Jenni Murray from*
> Woman's Hour.

JENNI MURRAY. And you can hear the full speech on the
Woman's Hour podcast, where we discuss fertility issues
among single working women –

> *The receptionist/office manager,* KIKI, *changes the radio*
> *station.* BRIDGET *enters, with gigantic shoulder bag,*
> *yelling into her mobile phone.*

BRIDGET. Goldman's? Fuck Goldman's. What's the floor?
Fuck it. Not at that price.

KIKI. Miss Parker? I'm afraid the doctor's running a tiny bit late.

BRIDGET. One minute. (*Mobile.*) It means TAKE YOUR
HANDS OFF YOUR COCKS AND STOP TRADING!
(*Mobile down.*) I'm going to have to reschedule. Office
emergency.

KIKI. We will have to charge a cancellation fee.

BRIDGET (*mobile rings*). It's fine, I'll pay it, tell him I'm
sorry. (*Into mobile.*) Not you, mate, you're fucked.

> *She hangs up, gathers her things.* KIKI *makes a call.*

KIKI. Dr Marshall? Wonderful speech. Your eleven-fifteen's
just cancelled. And Mr Price from Mansard Finance called
again about the valuation. He's suggesting lunch on Friday at
the Savoy Grill. See you shortly.

> *She hangs up.* BRIDGET *snaps to attention.*

BRIDGET. Mansard Finance?

KIKI. Sorry, that was a private message. Would you like to reschedule? The doctor's exceptionally busy right now so if you *did* want advice about sperm donors –

BRIDGET. I'll call. (*Mobile rings.*) Peter? I'm on my way. You'd better tape up your balls.

She exits.

JEFF. I'm amazed she can't find a man to impregnate her.

KIKI. Sorry about the wait. Doctor won't be long.

SERENA. Thank you.

JEFF. How was Drama Workshop?

SERENA. Feisty. Chantal was in the ADD one. Think of a character and describe them in three words. 'Childless psychotic old hag.' That's very imaginative, I said, how old is she? 'Forty.'

JEFF. That's four words.

SERENA. What?

JEFF. Childless psychotic old hag is four words. And you're thirty-five.

SERENA. Today is not the day to be literal, Jeff.

JEFF. How would you like me to be?

SERENA. Open-minded and quietly supportive.

JEFF. Should I tape my balls up, too?

MARSHALL *enters, talking on his mobile, and takes a file from* KIKI.

MARSHALL (*on phone*). No, I'll come on my motorbike straight from the clinic. I'll meet you at the Garrick at six.

He ushers SERENA *and* JEFF *into the consulting room and seats them.*

Mr and Mrs Robertson-Goswami. How wonderfully modern. Sorry I'm so backed up today, my conference ran over.

I'm sorry to see you here, too, nothing personal of course. Why don't you tell me a bit about yourselves.

SERENA. We've been trying for three years. Our first round of IVF failed. We didn't qualify for a second on the NHS so we went private, first to Life, then to Creation but nothing worked so we thought we'd try you. You had glowing testimonials.

JEFF. They all had glowing testimonials.

MARSHALL. There's a clinic out there to suit everyone. (*Consults the file.*) Two successful embryo transfers in four rounds of IVF, two miscarriages at six and seven weeks.

SERENA. I struggle to get pregnant. If I get pregnant I miscarry.

MARSHALL. I see. You have no prior children?

JEFF. I do. My daughter from a previous… Zara. She's away at uni.

MARSHALL. You must have had her young.

JEFF. I was twenty.

MARSHALL. Congratulations. Good general health? Working professionals?

SERENA. I'm an educational therapist. Jeff's a social worker.

MARSHALL. I'm honoured to have you. Sex life normal?

SERENA. Yes.

JEFF. Well –

MARSHALL. Cyclist, are you? Good for the lungs, less so for the sperm. Try fast walking.

SERENA (*to* JEFF). I told you.

MARSHALL. No family medical problems?

SERENA. Not in mine. Jeff's adopted. We don't know his history.

JEFF. I was raised by white parents. Have you ever met a black man called Jeff?

MARSHALL. Is adoption an option for you?

JEFF. No.

MARSHALL. Understandable. And you've not considered using donor eggs?

SERENA. We went on a waiting list but there were no Asian donors.

JEFF. We want a baby who looks like both of us.

MARSHALL. God made man in his own image, and so with human procreation. Not to worry. We'll start by running the usual tests and see what comes back.

JEFF. Can I –

SERENA (*a warning*). Jeff...

JEFF. It's just we've paid for three sets of the same tests in two different clinics. Why can't you use the existing ones?

MARSHALL. Clinic protocol. We have to ensure we give you the most accurate diagnosis. I hope our results speak for themselves.

SERENA. He got a princess pregnant.

MARSHALL. Princesses are made of tubes and cells just like you and me. There is no one-size-fits-all with IVF but I can promise you won't get a more bespoke treatment anywhere else.

JEFF. That sounds expensive.

MARSHALL. I understand it's difficult to quantify the value of human life.

JEFF. We're selling our car to pay for this. That's pretty quantifiable.

SERENA. Jeff!

MARSHALL. I sense a resistance. Remember, it only takes one egg and one sperm.

SERENA. He's not resistant. Just –

JEFF. Realistic. We've heard the one about the 'one egg' before. And that it's only a matter of time. I thought if were paying over the odds we might get some more original rhetoric.

SERENA *is mortified.* MARSHALL *gets up and sits on the desk.*

MARSHALL. I always wanted to be a great disco dancer but I was born with two left feet. All those nights I spent watching the pretty girls pair off with the snake-hipped and the lithe. Eventually I realised I was better at studying anatomy than worrying about my own.

SERENA. Jeff's a good disco dancer.

JEFF. A very good disco dancer.

MARSHALL. I envy you. What I'm saying is that we must work with what you've got. A good womb, clear tubes and decent sperm. We can stimulate egg growth and boost your chances, but I can't manufacture intention. I believe it's everyone's right to be a parent... but you must believe in your rights, too.

A shaft of sunlight shines through the window, illuminating him. A faint harp glissando plays. SERENA *smiles, rapt.*

SERENA. We do. (*To* JEFF.) Don't we?

JEFF *doesn't answer. The sunlight fades.* MARSHALL *addresses* JEFF.

MARSHALL. I don't say this lightly – but I think you've both got the human resources to see this through. That's just as important as money. All you need now is a little faith.

SERENA. He's our last chance. Please, Jeff.

JEFF *takes* SERENA*'s hand.*

JEFF. Okay.

MARSHALL. Kiki in reception will give you an information pack. Diet, supplements, relaxation exercises. Oh, and without wanting to make assumptions – saliva contains digestive enzymes that have a very damaging effect on sperm – so you might want to rethink your foreplay. See you at your next cycle. (*To* JEFF.) And try to go easy on yours.

Scene Three

Same day. BRIDGET *stands outside* LARISSA*'s office door, on her mobile. She takes off her trainers, takes a pair of heels out of her handbag and puts them on as she talks. We see* MILES *on the phone with her.*

BRIDGET. You'll be fine, babe. Just don't break out into any cabaret numbers, they'll never guess you're a sodomite.

MILES. Really? I feel like I've got a rainbow tattooed on my forehead.

LARISSA (*off*). Ready for you.

BRIDGET. I've got to go, Miles, I'm in with the COO. Good luck.

She hangs up and slaps herself round the face a few times, hard. She takes a breath and enters. LARISSA, *Australian, sits.* BRIDGET *stands.*

LARISSA. Ten years ago I would have offered you a stiff drink. I can't say I miss the old culture, but between you and me I cannot stand the taste of coconut water. Well? What are we looking at?

BRIDGET. About five mill in the hole. All the research said LifeSpan was solid.

LARISSA. LifeSpan. I'm not sure how I feel about stem cells. Making medicine from embryos?

BRIDGET. The market felt fine about it until someone leaked the drug trials.

LARISSA. I hear you stopped the traders' play.

BRIDGET. It was getting emotional.

LARISSA. When the odds diminish so do rational decisions. Where were you when it kicked off?

BRIDGET. Emergency root canal.

LARISSA. You couldn't get an after-hours?

BRIDGET. Look, it's my bad. But there's no way I could have foreseen the leak, Larissa.

LARISSA. We both know how little it takes to spook the market. I'd be more worried about the Motherfuckers upstairs.

BRIDGET. I'll make it up to you.

LARISSA. Good. Here's news. David's moving out.

BRIDGET. Really? Poached?

LARISSA. Hitched. Japanese. He showed me a picture. Like a porcelain doll. The kind you want to smash.

BRIDGET. Where's he going, Tokyo?

LARISSA. Hong Kong. Guess who's been asked to fill his boots. (*Flexes her muscles.*) Mamafucker. First woman in the boardroom.

BRIDGET. Congratulations.

LARISSA. I'd like to think it's my rapacious talent that got me the gig, not my snapper. But who cares?

BRIDGET. So… who's going to fill *your* boots?

LARISSA. That's my girl. Quick on the draw. Do you want it?

BRIDGET. Yes.

LARISSA. No hesitation.

BRIDGET. I want it. I really want it.

LARISSA. That's what I like about you, Bridget. You've been in the trenches. You survived the crash, dug in your – (*A glance at* BRIDGET*'s shoes.*) Louboutin heels through the recovery… and you're still hungry. These new recruits with their ethics and their MBAs and their *prudence* – underneath their Thomas Pink double-cuff split-yoke shirts, their flesh is running wet.

BRIDGET. Once you show the beast your fear, you're dead.

LARISSA. So, then. You'll need to show them – (*A nod upstairs.*) *us* – how much you deserve it.

BRIDGET. Have you heard of Genesis Incorporated? Private fertility clinic.

LARISSA. Why?

BRIDGET. Don't worry, I'm not in the market for a baby right now. But they are. The MD's very high profile – Joseph Marshall. He's all about women's reproductive rights. Especially egg freezing.

LARISSA. I'm not sure I buy it, darling. Call me a champagne feminist, but being able to breed until you're fifty isn't going to break the glass ceiling. That'll only happen when us girls get the chance to earn the same as men.

BRIDGET. This is a chance. I've just found out he wants to float the clinic. Mansard are doing a valuation. I'd like to pitch for it too.

LARISSA. Mansard have a pretty good history in biotech.

BRIDGET. So do I. Between us... I had my eggs frozen at Genesis last year.

LARISSA. That was the weepy period? I thought you were having an abortion, you sly dog. Did it work?

BRIDGET. I've got eight eggs in the bank. Not bad for my age. There's a twelve per cent chance of success per egg.

LARISSA. Darling, it was hardly worth it.

BRIDGET. It was to me. It's bought me time.

LARISSA. Well don't leave it too long, it gets murky down there after forty-five.

BRIDGET. It's big business. Freezing, IVF, genetic screening – Marshall's on the hard sell. He'll be the first to float but not the last. I know I could ace a pitch – I'm a first-hand consumer.

LARISSA. A hot IPO's always a good way to keep the Motherfuckers sweet. All right. Put it together and bring me your proposal.

BRIDGET. Thanks, Larissa. I appreciate it.

LARISSA. No sweat, darling. Right, John Lewis; the Mecca of the colonial classes.

She takes off her heels and puts on a pair of trainers.

BRIDGET. Retail therapy?

LARISSA. In John Lewis, are you kidding? No, birthday gift for Hugo. The higher up you marry in this country the less you have to spend. (*Leaving.*) Is that irony? Or are you guys just cheap?

Scene Four

Music room, St Brice's. MILES *is at the piano, playing and singing a hymn.*

MILES. He's got the whole world in his hands
He's got the whole world in his hands
He's got the whole world in his hands

A school bell rings somewhere signaling the end of the day. A voice on the Tannoy:

TANNOY. Will all staff please stay behind for the 4 p.m. fire drill. Boys attending French Club will now meet in the Joan of Arc Games Room. Thank you and '*au revoir*'.

MILES *segues into 'Non Je Ne Regrette Rien' and sings theatrically, amusing himself. A young trainee school priest, * FATHER SCALES, *comes to the door and stands watching. He's in civvies, his dog collar hidden by a scarf, and carries a bunch of keys.*

MILES *sings for a few bars, high camp, without noticing him.*

FATHER SCALES. You must be our new assistant music teacher.

MILES *stops playing.*

MILES. Yes. Hi. I'm Miles. Just trying out some ideas for the end-of-term recital. Something for the dads, as the Dean said.

FATHER SCALES. The Piaf might be a bit high for your altos.

MILES (*surprised*). Are you a fan?

FATHER SCALES. Aren't we all?

MILES. You're probably right, Orlando's voice is about to break. Travis and Bono aren't far behind.

FATHER SCALES. My school was more Andrews and Pauls.

MILES. Mine was Kevins and Steves. An unusually hirsute Brian. Prissy little things, Brians. Always the last to get a girlfriend.

FATHER SCALES. I'm a Brian myself.

MILES. Well done, Miles.

FATHER SCALES. I'm assuming you weren't named after Saint Miles Gerard the Catholic martyr.

MILES (*laughs*). The trumpet player. My father was a fan. And a Jew. Not that I advertise the fact here, of course. They don't take on non-Catholics here, do they?

FATHER SCALES. Not many. But I admire the Jews. They're survivors. It's hard to find peace in exile.

MILES. They certainly found a piece of me.

He makes a snipping motion, waits for FATHER SCALES *to laugh. He doesn't.*

So… what do I need to know? Walk, don't run, no holding hands in the refectory?

FATHER SCALES. Sorry?

MILES. You are the caretaker, right? They told me you'd find me after lessons to run through health and safety.

FATHER SCALES *removes his scarf, revealing a dog collar. He offers his hand.*

FATHER SCALES. I'm Father Scales, the trainee chaplain.

MILES. Oh. Christ! Sorry! Ah. It's just you're so… young.

FATHER SCALES. That's flattering.

MILES. I'm only half-Jewish, of course. (*A joke.*) And I've got very Catholic taste in music, it comes from my days in cabaret.

Jazz, ballads… I did a stint on a cruise ship once – tough audience. (*Sweating now*.) I feel very privileged to be here.

FATHER SCALES. There is a place for secular music at St Brice's, of course. But faith is always at the very heart of everything we do. Miles Gerard was hanged, drawn and quartered for his.

MILES (*inspiration strikes*). Actually my fiancée's Catholic. Bridget.

FATHER SCALES. A fiancée? That's a lovely name. Gentle St Brigid who worked among the lepers.

MILES. Mine's a charity worker. Very sweet girl.

FATHER SCALES. She'll be coming to the concert?

MILES. Of course.

FATHER SCALES. I'll look forward to meeting her. Enjoy your first week of term. And please, call me Brian.

Scene Five

Two weeks later. SHARON's living room. SHARON, fifties, picks up scattered toys. Her finger is bandaged with a splint. JEFF sits, with a file.

JEFF. I just want you to be aware of your rights.

SHARON. What about my right to keep my business private?

JEFF. Your neighbours heard everything, Sharon.

SHARON. Nosy bastards.

JEFF. They were worried about you.

SHARON. They've been trying to get rid of us since my daughter moved back in with her kids.

JEFF. So there's six of you now, including Grace, your youngest. That must be a lot of work.

SHARON. I'm not scared of work. Where's Brendan, anyway? I got Brendan last time.

JEFF. Brendan's on leave.

SHARON. Breakdown was it? Too soft for your game. Hands like a bishop.

JEFF. Brendan's fine, let's talk about Ron. Why did he hit you?

SHARON. Who says he hit me? He punched the wall. I got in the way.

JEFF. I thought Brendan made him do an anger-management course?

SHARON. Yeah. Didn't get him a job, did it. Look, he has a drink and then he gets in a mood. I feel sorry for him really.

JEFF. Physical abuse is against the law, however impotent he might feel.

SHARON. He ain't impotent, is he, we've got four kids.

JEFF. Has Ron ever hurt Grace, or the grandchildren?

SHARON. Don't be stupid. Ron's the one who takes care of them while I'm at work. I look after other people's children. They can afford me cos I don't speak French and I don't send pictures of their kids having a shit so they can give them marks out of ten. Ron picks ours up from nursery, gets their tea. And Grace can take care of herself.

JEFF. She's thirteen.

SHARON. School had her putting condoms on a banana. When I was her age it was up to the man to sort all that out. Didn't look nothing like a banana.

She cackles.

JEFF. Sharon, it's your right to live without fear of violence.

SHARON. Will you stop going on about my fucking rights? What's the point of rights if you can't afford them? You middle classes never get it.

JEFF. I'm not middle class. And it's better if we're honest with each other.

SHARON. All right. Look. His temper's got worse since he's been out of work. But do I look like a victim to you?

JEFF. I'm not saying you're a victim –

SHARON. Good. Because right now we've got an arrangement. I'm paying him not to touch me. So he can't have done it, can he?

JEFF. What?

SHARON. You heard. It's a business deal. Keeps him in beer money and out of my hair.

JEFF. By allowing Ron to monetise his failure to control himself?

SHARON. Eh?

JEFF. You're paying for something that you're morally entitled to get for free. How is that fair?

SHARON. Who said it was fair? I earn my money, I can spend it on what I want. It's a free-market economy, isn't it?

JEFF. It's madness, Sharon.

SHARON. That's capitalism for you, love. Your little face. I'm not middle class, my arse.

Scene Six

Same night. SERENA *and* JEFF*'s bedroom.* SERENA *sits on her bed, injecting hormones into her stomach with a hypodermic syringe.*

Elsewhere: BRIDGET*'s living room.* MILES *is at* BRIDGET*'s piano, playing and singing.* BRIDGET*'s bag sits on top of the piano.* BRIDGET *is on the sofa looking at her laptop.*

MILES. She's got the whole world in her bag
        She's got the whole world in her bag
        She's got the whole world in her bag
        She's got the whole world in her bag

He segues into a different song.

It's embossed by Gucci and lined with silk
It's home to spare knickers and almond milk
It's a Trojan horse, a Pandora's box
Carrying books from the school of hard knocks

It rattles with bones and vitamin pills
And when its shadow falls children run for the hills
Its aim is true, its mission is clear:
To deter any man from coming too near

Yes it says, here is a woman who's paid off her loans
With friends in high places with holiday homes
Yeah she does yoga retreats and monthly therapy
But she's hearing the tick-tock-tick of biology

BRIDGET *applauds.* MILES *stays at the piano and noodles on it through the next, making notes in his notebook.*

JEFF *and* SERENA's *bedroom.* JEFF *enters the bedroom eating ice cream from the tub.*

JEFF. Okay in here? (*Sees the needle, recoils.*) I'll come back.

SERENA *calmly withdraws the needle from her stomach.*

SERENA. Do. Not. Move. (*Prepares a second syringe.*) Some men actually inject their wives for them.

She injects again, winces. JEFF *closes his eyes and sits down on the bed, back turned.*

JEFF. You know how I am about needles.

SERENA. Last night you watched a man get his leg chewed off in *Shark Attack*. And eighteen years ago you stood down the business end and saw your daughter shred your girlfriend's vagina like a Chinese cabbage. Deal with it!

JEFF. My ex-girlfriend's vagina.

SERENA *stands up, brandishing the needle.*

SERENA. Shall I stab this in your eye? Maybe that'd cure your phobia.

JEFF *retreats to the other side of the room with the ice cream.*

We're supposed to be on a cleanse. No dairy or sugar.

JEFF. I'm hungry.

SERENA. I made Dr Marshall's fertility lasagne.

JEFF. You made lasagne.

SERENA. I made lasagne with tomatoes which are full of lycopene to help produce healthy sperm.

JEFF. I cleansed all week. Tonight I want to be dirty.

SERENA. That's good.

JEFF (*hopeful*). Yeah?

SERENA. Yeah. You shouldn't abstain for more than seven days before the egg retrieval. Go and sort yourself out.

JEFF *sits on the bed with the ice cream. During the next* SERENA *puts her hormones away and sits on the bed with a laptop.*

BRIDGET*'s flat.* MILES *continues performing.*

MILES. She'll wait no more for a suitable guy
From now on it's DIY
She's banked her eggs and she's hedging her wealth
In stocks and shares she's made of herself

So there'll be no more going through the mill
No there'll be no more blind dates and birth-control pills
Now she's closed her accounts for both Tinder and Match
Though to keep up morale she still waxes her –

BRIDGET. You wouldn't dare.

MILES. I'm thinking for the end-of-term concert, since you're my guest.

BRIDGET. Do I have to?

MILES. You're my Catholic beard. I've got to stay in Brian's good books while I'm on new-teacher probation.

BRIDGET. He can't sack you for being gay.

MILES. You don't know how strict this school is. Every time I open my mouth something heretical falls out.

BRIDGET. I'm from Essex, babe. How's that going to improve your status?

MILES. You have the sheen of a successful career woman on you. You'll make me look kosher.

BRIDGET. Jew.

MILES. Half-Jew. How's the sperm search going?

BRIDGET. It's not for me, it's research for the clinic valuation. I'm pitching on Monday. Still haven't nailed my angle.

MILES. Let's see. (*Takes the laptop.*) Caucasian-Ukrainian, ninety-three kilos, eyes blue, hair brown, retail butcher.

BRIDGET. Is there any other kind?

MILES. Maybe he gives away sausages in his spare time. It says he likes rock climbing and cats and he's a skilled first-aider. Useful. Can we see what he looks like?

BRIDGET. No. They charge twenty-five quid for a photo and it's only of him as a kid. I just need to know how much they're selling his wares for.

MILES. Four hundred and fifty quid a straw. There are worse ways to make a living.

BRIDGET. They don't get paid for it, babe. That's why they're called donors. It's just expenses.

MILES. Travel card, Wet Wipes, copy of *Razzle*. And the women have to pay for it through the nose.

BRIDGET. Four fifty's cheap. The British Cryo Bank charges nine hundred. Plus carriage. Plus storage. Plus washing.

MILES. I could be your sperm-washer. Remember Daniel, my boyfriend at uni? He had a summer job washing cashmere jumpers for a member of Pink Floyd. I always wondered what it led to, career-wise.

BRIDGET. I don't remember Daniel. In my college memories you're heterosexual.

MILES. You were my last hurrah. I spent my first gay summer with Dan. While you were temping at Credit Suisse.

BRIDGET. I had to do something, seeing as I didn't have a dick.

MILES. His hardly qualified as one.

BRIDGET *takes the laptop away from him.*

I still don't get it. Last month you'd finally decided to go for the big defreeze and now you're flogging your doctor's business?

BRIDGET. New game plan, babe.

MILES. Talk me through it.

BRIDGET. I get the pitch, handle the IPO, give the Motherfuckers upstairs a hard-on and bag a massive end-of-year bonus. Then I secretly get pregnant before the end of the financial year so they have to include the bonus when they calculate my maternity pay.

MILES. Conservative estimate?

BRIDGET. If the float does well... five hundred K? That'd take my maternity to about... a hundred and fifteen grand a week before tax for the first six weeks. How's that for a kiss-my-arse?

MILES. You do know if you fuck them over you won't be able to go back afterwards.

BRIDGET. I don't want to go back. I'm done with banking.

MILES. You've been saying that for five years.

BRIDGET. Same amount of time you've been saying you'll buy a flat and get your own piano.

MILES. I'm nearly there. Got my deposit, just about. Cleared my debts. I just need three months' payslips and a kind mortgage broker and I'll become a fully qualified adult.

BRIDGET. I said I'd lend you the rest of your deposit.

MILES. Thanks, angel, but no more debts to the Bank of Bridget. That's the whole point of owning a house, not sharing a mouldy flat with three nurses and a communal epilator. Same reason you put your eggs on ice.

BRIDGET. I was running out of time.

MILES. Yeah. But it's about staying in control, really, isn't it? Having agency, as my therapist used to say, before she moved to Kent.

BRIDGET. Maybe. I hadn't thought about it like that.

MILES. You should put that in your pitch. If you win you can give me a bonus.

JEFF *and* SERENA*'s bedroom.* SERENA *is scrolling on her laptop.*

JEFF. Fertility Forum, is it?

SERENA. They know what I'm going through.

JEFF. How can you tell?

JEFF *grabs the computer, reads a thread.*

'TTC 4 6 2 IVF 3 MC.'

SERENA. 'Trying to conceive for six years, two in vitro, three miscarriages.'

JEFF. 'DP HE BIH 4.'

SERENA. 'Dear partner's had enough but I'm holding out for – '

JEFF. 'A BFP AIBU?'

SERENA. – 'a big fat positive, am I being unreasonable.'

JEFF. Y.

SERENA. It makes me feel part of a community.

JEFF. A community of failure? It's like a catalogue of death. You know I saw a new client today. She's paying her husband not to beat her up.

SERENA. So?

JEFF. So this woman feels so worthless after thirty years with a violent man that she gives him money not to abuse her. He profits from his own dysfunction and she swallows the cost to keep the peace. I told her she's mad, but who are we to talk?

SERENA. I have no idea what you're talking about, Jeff.

JEFF. Think about it. Normal fertility is actually worthless to a doctor like Marshall. It's our biological dysfunction that holds the value, which is why he benefits every time we don't get pregnant.

SERENA. He will get us pregnant.

JEFF. How do you know?

SERENA. Because I have faith in him.

JEFF. What you mean is, you have faith in money.

SERENA. He told us we've got what it takes.

JEFF. Yes, so that if he fails, we believe it's our fault for not being good enough. A Marxist would call that false consciousness.

SERENA. Can we please leave Marx out of this? Go to sleep. Put a bolster down the middle of the bed if it makes you happier.

JEFF. What would make me happy is to get naked under the covers and kiss like we used to, and then maybe fuck like a normal couple. (*Beat.*) I miss your pussy.

SERENA. Don't call it that.

JEFF. You used to like it.

SERENA. A pussy isn't a babymaker, it's a parking space for a spray-tanned porn star's meat-hammer.

JEFF. Fine, I miss your birth canal, your semen aqueduct, your womb estuary. But once again it's full of men in waders setting lobster traps or AIB un-fucking-reasonable?

She starts to cry. JEFF *watches, emotionless.*

When you cry I don't feel anything any more.

SERENA *snatches up the ice cream. She starts to smear it over* JEFF's *face.*

SERENA. Feel that?

JEFF *tries to push her off.* SERENA *mashes ice cream into his hair.*

JEFF. You're insane.

SERENA. You'd be insane if you'd had two children die inside you.

JEFF. They were embryos, not children. Clumps of cells.

SERENA. They were *our* cells, until you stopped wanting them to grow.

They struggle on the bed.

JEFF. They didn't grow because your body rejected them, not because I didn't believe in them. You can't have science *and* magic, they're mutually exclusive.

SERENA *spits in his face.*

SERENA. It's positive intention! That's physics, not magic. (*A beat.*) Why can't you dream with me?

Scene Seven

Three weeks later. BRIDGET *and* MARSHALL *in his consulting room.*

BRIDGET. Australia, 2013. A leading private fertility clinic floats on the ASX, retaining twenty-eight per cent of the company. They issue stock at a very reasonable five dollars sixty-eight cents which hits a fifty-two-week high of nine dollars twenty cents before stabilising at sixty cents below. Total generated profit... three hundred and forty-five million dollars.

MARSHALL. The figures are impressive.

BRIDGET. The market demand for assisted conception seems infinite. I understand there's no government regulation of private fees.

MARSHALL. No.

BRIDGET. And you're making an average mark-up on treatment of around, say – four hundred per cent.

MARSHALL. It sounds like a lot, doesn't it.

BRIDGET. Like you said, the figures are impressive. I'm guessing that your client list will only get bigger as the NHS keep withdrawing funding for IVF.

MARSHALL. There's the irony. The NHS hospitals who do still give free IVF are entirely reliant on their private patients to pay for it. Medicine and profit are not mutually exclusive, nor can they afford to be, not any more.

BRIDGET. Even better, IVF only works roughly thirty per cent of the time for your average client. Egg freezing at my age, even less. For the seventy per cent failures, you're still in profit. It's a pretty unique market position.

MARSHALL. Well yes, if you put it like that.

BRIDGET. I do. And we are the best firm to underwrite your IPO.

MARSHALL. You've certainly got first-hand experience of my clinical expertise.

BRIDGET. But…

MARSHALL. Is this too close to home for you to give me an objective assessment of my business? Mansard Finance have been trading in my sector for twenty years.

BRIDGET. True. But I can tell you this. The trading desk at Mansard is one hundred per cent male. So is their sales team. They're the ones who'll have to go out and convince investors to buy your stock. They may be good businessmen, but they don't know the true value of your company. I do. When I froze my eggs with you I felt in control. Not punished by biology.

MARSHALL. I admire how sanguine you are about your own
    situation, Miss Parker.

BRIDGET. Dr Marshall, that's why I can make your buyers see
    they're investing in far more than just another biotech stock.
    They're giving real agency to women just like me.

MARSHALL. Call me Joseph.

They shake hands.

Scene Eight

SERENA *lies in bed, listening to a relaxation tape on her
headphones.*

NARRATOR. You are feeling deeply relaxed. Deeply, deeply,
    deeply relaxed. You're ready to enter your sacred space. Can
    you see the door? Good. It's a beautiful door. It's *your* door.
    Now push it open and walk inside. Congratulations. You
    have journeyed to the inside of your womb. The chamber in
    which your child will grow. Take a minute to appreciate it.
    Is it a welcoming space?

SERENA *nods.*

Good. Now listen. Does your womb want to say anything
    to you?

*A burst of radio static. A voice speaks. It is Jenni Murray
from* Woman's Hour.

WOMB. In the 1960s women fought for liberation from
    domestic slavery. Their daughters have deferred having
    children for the sake of their careers, sometimes leaving it
    too late. Is this progress? Or the great tragedy of feminism?

SERENA *sits up.*

SERENA. You're my womb? You sound very familiar.

WOMB. Good. I aim for gravitas, but with sisterly warmth.

SERENA. So is it going to work this time? Has my embryo taken?

WOMB. I'm afraid I can't comment. The others will blame me if something goes wrong.

SERENA. What others?

WOMB. Who do you think grew the eggs? Just don't get your birth canal involved, or she'll never shut up.

SERENA. Can she talk too?

VAGINA (*Indian accent*). Who's she, the cat's mother?

SERENA. Mum?

VAGINA. If you'd paid me a little more attention perhaps we wouldn't be having all these problems now.

SERENA. My eggs aren't good. Nobody said anything about my nunu.

VAGINA. You infantilise me and still expect me to do my holy work?

SERENA. You're just the exit route. It's my womb who grows the embryo. Right?

OVARIES (*two voices, very faint*). So hierarchical.

SERENA. Hello?

WOMB. Ovaries. They're very weak right now.

OVARIES. Compromised fallopian tubes, insufficient ova.

SERENA. Did I do something wrong?

WOMB. We hardly know ourselves any more.

OVARIES. Hostile uterine environment, incompetent cervical mucus –

VAGINA. Womb versus ovaries, good eggs versus baddies –

WOMB. There is no whole. Only the anomie. Of total –

MARX (*off*). Alienation.

SERENA. Who's that?

WOMB. Today's guest. Some of you will know him simply as the great thinker with the big beard.

SERENA. God?

KARL MARX *enters the bedroom*.

MARX. You flatter me, my dear.

SERENA. Karl Marx? Who invited you in here?

MARX. You did, *liebchen*. Your subconscious mind knows full well that you are fighting a new enemy.

SERENA. Who, Jeff?

MARX. *Nein*. Ask yourself, who controls the means of human production in this age of advanced capitalism? Not God. Not women. *Die* bourgeois *Doktoren*.

WOMB. Nice segway.

MARX. *Danke*.

SERENA. Can we keep politics out of my uterus, please?

MARX. Without politics there can be no revolution – this is something women do not like to face.

OVARIES. Excuse me. We fought a revolution over fifty years ago.

VAGINA. A little invention called the pill.

OVARIES. And legal recourse to abortion.

WOMB. Ouch. You did that on purpose.

WOMB, OVARIES *and* VAGINA *start to squabble*.

OVARIES. We didn't.

VAGINA. They did.

WOMB. Stay out of this, you jumped-up waterchute.

VAGINA. I am the sacred *yoni*, embodiment of the goddess Shakti and the origin of life itself! Mess with the cosmos and you'll wither and die, bitch.

WOMB. There's sisterhood for you.

SERENA. Can everyone shut up a minute?

Her organs ignore this and keep muttering insults quietly during the next.

MARX. You see? Your idea of sexual equality was to sacrifice your reproductive rights to the needs of the bankers and factory owners. And now you are forced to buy them back at inflated prices. It is no surprise that your organs have turned against each other.

SERENA. So it's only going to work if we pull together?

MARX. *Genau, genau.* You must unite your reproductive workforce.

OVARIES. Have you seen what we're up against? Hormones, needles.

VAGINA. Metal probes wielded by men in rubber gloves. It's a war zone.

SERENA. Can't you be a bit more positive? Have some faith in each other, and in me.

WOMB. Well, girls?

OVARIES. We'll do our best, dear.

VAGINA. Just as long as I'm put to good use again. Will I see a penis any time soon?

SERENA. I can't promise that. I have to do what Dr Marshall advises.

MARX. Wait! That is not what I said. You must mount a revolution *against* the system that oppresses you.

SERENA. Yes, I know – biology.

MARX. *Nein, nein…* against the babymakers. Charismatic men of science whose goal above all is profit.

WOMB. But we can't get pregnant without science.

MARX. I agree, it is a dialectic without solution. I can only diagnose the problem, not solve it.

OVARIES. Typical mansplaining.

SERENA. Yeah, I paid for a positive visualisation, not a lecture from a dead white man.

MARX. A little anger, *gut*. First there is smoke, then fire.

SERENA. Oh FUCK OFF and patronise someone else.

WOMB. Melvyn Bragg's in the Green Room, reading his own novel.

MARX. Modern women are so caustic. Melvyn!

He disappears. 'The Internationale' plays faintly – interrupted by a burst of static.

SERENA. Ignore him. The ball's in your court now, womb. Please be a good host to my embryo.

VAGINA. And remember, *beti*, nothing goes in or out without me.

NARRATOR. Can you picture the new life growing inside you? Good. Is there anything you'd like to say to your child?

SERENA clasps her stomach.

SERENA. Yes. I believe in you. I believe in you. I believe in you…

A quick pulse of sound – laughing children, at play.

Scene Nine

Three weeks later. July. JEFF and SERENA in the clinic waiting room.

JEFF. I'm sorry.

SERENA. Don't lie. You're relieved.

JEFF. I'm relieved we know. It's been torture, watching you go through this again.

SERENA. The torture's just beginning.

KIKI enters with a glass of water for SERENA.

KIKI. For what it's worth… my sister got pregnant naturally after three rounds of IVF.

SERENA. This was our fifth.

KIKI. Five or six rounds is quite common before successful conception –

JEFF. We can't afford another round.

KIKI. You'd be amazed how many people find the money. Loans, credit cards… one client sold her entire shoe collection on eBay.

SERENA. He's got money for his daughter's education. He just won't give it to me.

JEFF. Let's go home and talk about it there.

SERENA. Let's talk about it now. I want a witness.

JEFF. Sorry. There was a lot riding on this one.

KIKI. I understand. While we're waiting – (*Produces a credit card machine*.) I do have to process payment for the services you just had.

JEFF. How much were today's services?

KIKI. It's one-fifty for the follow-up appointment, seventy for the blood test, and twenty for the pregnancy test.

JEFF. We bought our own pregnancy test. It was three quid.

KIKI. Sorry, it's clinic protocol.

SERENA. You see? He's tight. Except when it concerns Zara and the ex-girlfriend.

JEFF. The ex-girlfriend who raped my sperm?

SERENA. Rape?

JEFF. Tricking a man into getting you pregnant, why not?

   KIKI *hands the credit card machine to* JEFF *so he can enter his PIN.*

KIKI. Actually, rape is nonconsensual sexual intercourse.

JEFF. What about nonconsensual conception? How many men do you think get trapped into fatherhood every year?

KIKI. To be clear, sir, it's not rape. (*Tears off the receipt.*) So that's two hundred and forty pounds, thank you very much.

JEFF. The water's free then?

KIKI. Dr Marshall is the best consultant in the industry. Statistically speaking.

JEFF. I just spent seven grand on the basis of his statistics. That's a thousand more than we budgeted for, what with all the blood tests and add-ons and baby lasagnes. So why isn't my wife pregnant?

KIKI. I'm afraid we can't give any guarantees, obviously.

JEFF. So what's the wall of baby pictures for? That's if they're even real.

KIKI. I can assure you that all the babies in those pictures were born to our clients. Although not all from the London clinic.

JEFF. He's got another clinic?

KIKI. Yes, in Surrey. We're hoping to expand to Dubai.

JEFF. The only thing that's guaranteed to breed in this world is money.

SERENA. Don't waste your breath. He's a man. He has no idea what I'm going through.

JEFF. Because I don't have ovaries? That's fair.

SERENA. It isn't fucking fair. You should try being a woman some time.

JEFF. If we're on to suffering league tables, try being adopted.

SERENA. Try being a social pariah.

JEFF. Try being a black man.

SERENA. Try being a brown girl.

KIKI. Perhaps you'd like to book a session with our counseller, Dr Cho?

JEFF. No. No more counselling, no more propaganda. Let's go home.

SERENA. No.

JEFF. I'm not leaving you here.

SERENA. Why not?

JEFF. Because I love you. And they're probably charging us to sit here.

SERENA. If you don't want my children you don't love me enough.

JEFF. Who says I don't want your children?

SERENA. How can a baby attach to my womb when its father doesn't believe in it?

JEFF. It can't attach because you're infertile! Barren, unfruitful, sterile… whatever you want to call it. And it's not my fault I already have a daughter.

A beat.

SERENA. Just say it, Jeff.

JEFF. Say what?

SERENA. Say you don't want a baby with me.

JEFF. I'm not being forced into a corner here…

SERENA. If you want to help me, for God's sake, just say it.

JEFF. You're over-emotional, you're still pumped full of hormones –

KIKI (*threatening*). Say it.

A beat.

JEFF. I don't want a baby with you. Not like this. I'm sorry.

Scene Ten

BRIDGET*'s living room.* BRIDGET *pours champagne.*

BRIDGET. Here's to us.

MILES. To you.

BRIDGET. To you. And Genesis Incorporated.

MILES. You're not going to get too busy for me now, are you? You're still coming to the concert?

BRIDGET. I said I would.

MILES. Good. So, what happens next?

BRIDGET. We prepare the float and I prepare my exit strategy.

MILES. You're definitely pressing the red button.

BRIDGET. Yeah. As soon as my promotion's in the bag and I've found my donor.

MILES. I'll be your sperm agent. What sort of budget are we looking at?

BRIDGET. The sky's the limit for good genes. That's why there's a black market too.

MILES. For jizz?

BRIDGET. Oh yeah. Jam jars being handed over in car parks. Cash changing hands.

MILES. Shame I'm not selling.

BRIDGET. Shall I make you an offer?

MILES *laughs.* BRIDGET *doesn't.*

MILES. What?

BRIDGET. Nothing. Just…

MILES. Bridget?

BRIDGET. You're telling me it hasn't crossed your mind? Not even once?

MILES. Well… no. And… why haven't you asked before?

BRIDGET. You've hardly been in a position to be a parent till now. As soon as you stop being so stubborn you'll own your own flat.

MILES. Wait... so it's the mortgage that qualifies me?

BRIDGET. I'm just being practical. And you were always adamant you didn't want kids.

MILES. That was twenty years ago.

BRIDGET. Yes, it started when you 'reoriented'. Figures.

MILES. I'm sorry?

BRIDGET. Your sexuality is essentially... well, it's selfish.

MILES. Talk me through it.

BRIDGET. Okay. Not only do gay men have a self-imposed entitlement to fuck around – don't give me that holy face – you might not, but plenty do – but you're never going to put your cocks to an end that isn't entirely self-pleasing.

MILES. Holy shit.

BRIDGET. I have no problem with it, it's just a fact.

MILES. Plenty of gay men have kids.

BRIDGET. Name me one gay friend of yours with children.

MILES. Elton John.

BRIDGET. Knowing all the words to 'Your Song' does not make Elton John your friend.

MILES. I still don't see how being childless makes my sex drive any more selfish than your maternal instincts.

BRIDGET. Excuse me?

MILES. Be honest. Do you really want to be a parent or do you just want a baby to add to your portfolio?

BRIDGET. Fuck off. I wasn't ready before.

MILES. Nor was I.

BRIDGET. So you're telling me you *would* have a kid?

MILES. Maybe. If I could afford it.

BRIDGET. I'd be the one paying for everything.

MILES. I don't want a baby on hire purchase.

BRIDGET. You've been borrowing money off me for the last twenty years.

MILES. So I owe you back taxes, fine, *mea culpa*... but suddenly you want payment in *ejaculate*?

BRIDGET. Forget it, all right.

MILES. No. You've been spending too much time around rich people. Poverty's contagious and the rich stay immune by cultivating a tribal sense of entitlement.

BRIDGET. You're the one who's entitled – you just can't admit it.

MILES. Me? I'm broke, I'm forty, I'm a single gay half-Jew hiding in a sea of upstanding uncut Catholics –

BRIDGET. You've got SPERM, you dimwit! You're a fucking billionaire, you and all your asset-loaded jizz oligarchs. Only instead of sharing it around you just sit there gloating on your hordes like great greedy swollen-balled homo dragons.

MILES. I'm going to go now.

BRIDGET. It's Friday night. Nobody should be alone on Shabbat.

MILES. You won't be alone. There's a gigantic elephant in the room.

BRIDGET. Please. I don't want a butcher's child. I want one with someone I love.

ACT TWO

Scene One

SHARON*'s flat. She has a bruised eye, and is smoking a fag.*

JEFF. Looks like your deal with Ron stopped working.

He examines her eye.

SHARON. Ow! I changed the arrangement, didn't I.

JEFF. I suppose that's some sort of progress.

SHARON. Yeah. If he lashes out now, he's got to pay me a fine out of his dole money. Twenty-five quid a punch. Fifty for something serious, like if he pushed me downstairs.

JEFF. Let me get this straight –

SHARON. It was a good deterrent for a while, cos he's never got no money. Then the other night he gets pissed and gives me a slap. I make him pay up. Soon as the money's in my hand he does it again.

JEFF. Why?

SHARON. He didn't feel guilty no more. Said in future he'd rather pay the fine and do what he felt like. So I punched him in the face and suddenly he's asking *me* for money, the cheeky cunt.

JEFF *puts his head in his hands.*

What's the matter with you? You look like shit.

JEFF. I've not been sleeping well.

SHARON. Up all night worrying about me, are you?

She cackles.

JEFF. I've had to move out of home for a bit.

SHARON. Oh yeah? Been a naughty boy, have you?

JEFF. No. I was just honest with my wife. The truth hurts. People don't want to hear it, do they, Sharon?

SHARON. You're the one with all the answers, not me. Where you staying then?

JEFF. With my ex-girlfriend. In my daughter's old bedroom. (*Professional.*) Look, I think we should talk about some of the options open to us.

SHARON. Options?

JEFF. About taking you and the children to a place of safety.

SHARON. For fuck's sake. I told you, it's Ron who looks after our kids and grandkids. How's going to a place of fucking safety gonna help me put food on the table if I got to pay for my own childcare? (*A beat.*) Cat got your tongue?

JEFF. I'm trying to think of a metaphor to make you understand why you're letting Ron exploit you.

SHARON. Ooh, a metaphor. Brendan just brought HobNobs.

JEFF. Remember the bankers? The financial crash happened because brokers sold thousands of people mortgages they couldn't afford. But it was us, the homeowners and the taxpayers, who paid the real price. The banks felt they'd paid their dues and the whole system went on like before.

SHARON. It's a crap metaphor. I got the right to charge for what I'm good at. And that's taking care of kids and taking shit from Ron.

JEFF. Fine, it's your right. But what's it doing to your family?

SHARON. I swear to God, if you middle-class types weren't all so obsessed with ethics and metaphors you might think about your own kids a bit more instead of everyone else's. Oh sorry. I forgot. You're not middle class.

JEFF. All I do is think about kids. Including the one I just told my wife we shouldn't have.

SHARON. Maybe it's just as well. Maybe, 'metaphorically', Jeff, if you have a kid now it'll be mugs like me who end up paying for it.

JEFF. How?

SHARON. First off it'll probably have ADD or dyspraxia or whatever it is they call posh kids these days instead of just being thick, so it'll grow up with personality issues; second, you won't be able to afford to send it to university though why bother cos there won't be any jobs anyway so it'll never have the money to buy a house and rents will go up, unless it moves to the countryside, which is shit; and last you'll probably die before it's forty which means when it retires it'll be my great-grandkids having to wipe its arse on minimum wage.

A beat.

JEFF. So what are we supposed to do then?

SHARON. I dunno, love. Get a dog?

Scene Two

Clinic reception. MARSHALL *is about to leave the office and is on his mobile talking to* SERENA. *We see her on the call.*

SERENA. It's not physical pain. I can cope with that. It's this feeling that I'm being punished for something.

MARSHALL. Do you know the Old Testament story about Abraham and Sarah? They were both over ninety when Sarah conceived her son Isaac. A reward from God for their spiritual faith. But when a stranger made the prophecy, Sarah laughed. She thought she was being mocked.

SERENA. Are you saying I should start praying?

MARSHALL. I'm saying I want you to stop feeling ashamed of your desire to have children. It does not make you weak, or greedy, or unreasonable.

SERENA. So you'll take me back? If I can find the money?

The clinic phone rings – KIKI *answers.*

KIKI. Genesis Inc. Kiki speaking, how can I help?

MARSHALL. Of course. Between the two of us, the clinic is expanding. We're now offering two and three-cycle packages, and credit options.

KIKI (*to* MARSHALL). Bridget Parker on the line.

MARSHALL. Just a second. (*Into phone, to* SERENA.) Before you do anything, go and see your husband. Sarah was a very resilient lady. And your powers of persuasion might be stronger than you think.

SERENA. Thank you. Thank you so much.

MARSHALL. God bless. (*Hangs up and picks up the other phone*.) Bridget?

BRIDGET *appears, on the call.*

BRIDGET. We've registered the IPO. It's official, Joseph. You're going to market.

MARSHALL (*soberly*). Thank you.

He hangs up. A beat – then he throws a celebratory dance move and plants a kiss on KIKI's *face.*

Scene Three

Music room, evening. MILES *is in a suit, trying to do up his tie.* BRIDGET *watches. She has an even more gigantic new handbag.*

MILES. New bag?

BRIDGET. Promotion present from Larissa.

MILES. Congratulations. Just don't stand too close to Brian. You stink of champagne.

BRIDGET. Don't be a brat. I left my own celebration drinks to come here.

MILES. I'm nervous. Have you seen the parents in the audience?

BRIDGET. Yeah. It's like Hugo Boss and Prada sponsored *Songs of Praise*.

MILES. Oh, I nearly forgot.

He takes a ring out of his pocket.

BRIDGET. What the fuck is that?

MILES. Engagement ring. It's from a Marks and Spencer's Christmas cracker.

BRIDGET. You really pushed the boat out for me.

MILES *goes on wrestling with his tie.*

MILES. Fucking thing.

BRIDGET. Come here. (*Does up his tie.*) All this fuss for a priest who's probably a closet case himself?

MILES. I like him. I want him to see me in a different light.

BRIDGET. What, as a liar?

MILES. A respectable adult with a personal link to the Catholic church. I need them to renew my contract.

BRIDGET. Jesus.

MILES. You can't say that in here unless you mean it. Put the ring on.

BRIDGET. It's too small.

MILES. Spit?

BRIDGET. Hand cream.

She rummages in her bag.

He might be able to guarantee your soul but he can't guarantee your mortgage. I said I'd lend you the money.

MILES. I know what you said.

BRIDGET. And just to clarify, it's not in exchange for your 'you know what'.

MILES. Ah, my 'you know what'? Is this the final demand?

BRIDGET. I didn't demand anything, I asked you to think about it.

MILES. I am thinking about it. I can't *stop* thinking about it. Can you hurry up?

BRIDGET *keeps rummaging unsuccessfully.*

You know you'll never have time to look after a baby, not when you spend half your life elbow-deep in your It Bag like a vet rummaging in a cow's arse.

BRIDGET *finds the hand cream.* MILES *snatches it and squirts it on her hands.*

BRIDGET. Careful! It's Crème de la Mer.

MILES. You see? Your hand cream's worth more than I am.

FATHER SCALES *enters with a baby monitor.*

FATHER SCALES. I heard the warm-up. The boys are in fine voice tonight. You must be Bridget.

BRIDGET. You must be Brian.

MILES. Father Scales.

BRIDGET. I've heard lots about you, Father Scales.

BRIDGET *goes to curtsy, stops herself, sticks out her hand, drops the ring.* FATHER SCALES *picks it up and puts it on her ring finger. It just about goes on.*

FATHER SCALES. Careful now. It looks… valuable.

He wipes his hands surreptitiously.

BRIDGET. I don't need a big diamond. Miles is my rock. (*Kisses* MILES.) See you after. Good luck.

She leaves. FATHER SCALES *plugs in the baby monitor near the piano.*

FATHER SCALES. The assembly hall is packed to the gills.

MILES. Is that a baby monitor?

FATHER SCALES. Yes, I'm plugging you in so I can call you when it's time.

MILES. Is it yours?

FATHER SCALES. No, I'm not –

MILES. Married?

FATHER SCALES. Or a father.

MILES. Me neither. Bit of a bone of contention right now.

FATHER SCALES. With your fiancée?

MILES. Yeah. She's keen... I'm not so sure.

FATHER SCALES. I thought you'd seemed troubled lately.

MILES. Have I?

FATHER SCALES. A good priest develops a sixth sense about these things.

MILES. I suppose I've been wrestling with myself a bit. (*Quickly.*) Emotionally, not in a physical sense. I just can't decide what to do.

FATHER SCALES. You must trust God to guide you to make the right choice.

MILES. But if God remains... silent on the matter? I mean, speaking as an existentially self-questioning half non-Christian – right now I can only hear my own voice.

FATHER SCALES. What is it saying to you?

MILES. That if I give her what she wants I'll compromise our relationship. And if I refuse then I'm denying both of us the right to fulfil our human potential.

FATHER SCALES. Well, a child is a gift from God, not a right. Hard for a non-Catholic to understand, perhaps.

MILES. See, this is where I get stuck. Is it a gift? Or is it just some sort of narcissistic urge to leave a mark like the cavemen did? Isn't it enough to commit to living this life as well as you can without having to render a bison in clay paint when you're no good at art anyway?

FATHER SCALES. Interesting hypothesis.

MILES. My BA was in Music and Anthropology.

FATHER SCALES. The battle for spiritual logic is at the very heart of our faith. You'd have made a good Catholic yourself.

MILES. Thank you.

> FATHER SCALES *switches on the baby monitor. It crackles and whines.*

FATHER SCALES. We have lift-off. Just leave the mute button on so we can't hear you. And Miles.

MILES. Yes?

FATHER SCALES. Fatherhood is not for everyone. There are many ways to carry out God's work.

> *He leaves.* MILES *stays on stage and plays a warm-up.*

Scene Four

Same night. DAISY*'s flat.* JEFF *sits on a single bed, listening to music on headphones.*

DAISY *knocks and enters, wearing her dressing gown.*

DAISY. You look just like Zara sitting there.

JEFF. Checking out her music. At least I had one positive influence.

DAISY. Don't be so hard on yourself. (*Massages his shoulders.*) You should do yoga with me some time. You're carrying a lot of tension.

JEFF. I'm okay.

DAISY. Still no word from Serena?

JEFF. No.

DAISY. Give her time. She must be in a living hell right now.

JEFF. That's the nicest thing I've ever heard you say about her.

DAISY. No woman should have to choose between having a man and having a baby.

JEFF. That's not what she's doing, Daisy.

DAISY. Isn't it?

DAISY takes the headphones and listens in.

I remember this. Blue Note club. You with dreadlocks and a burning desire to change the world.

JEFF. I'm not that kid any more. Not that dreamer either.

DAISY. No? One day you'd walk into a train carriage or a waiting room and your mum would be sitting there. She'd tap you on the shoulder. 'I know you,' she'd say.

JEFF. We all know how that fantasy played out. No forwarding address.

DAISY *(touches him)*. Maybe that's why you don't want another baby. You need to heal your inner child. The one who's always searching for his true source.

She kisses him… JEFF resists. The headphones are pulled out of the stereo… music plays. DAISY starts to dance with JEFF. She kisses him again… this time he responds. She unzips his trousers – they fumble with each other for a bit. Then JEFF pushes her away and turns off the music.

Jeff?

JEFF. I can't.

DAISY. You need more time.

JEFF. That's not what I need.

The doorbell rings.

You'd better get that.

DAISY leaves. JEFF composes himself.

Elsewhere we hear FATHER SCALES on the baby monitor.

FATHER SCALES *(off)*. Miles to the stage please, this is your beginner's call.

DAISY comes back in with SERENA.

DAISY. I told her this wasn't a good time.

JEFF. What are you doing here?

SERENA. I wanted to ask you something.

JEFF. Okay…

He glances at DAISY *but she doesn't move.*

SERENA. Or should I come back when you're not so busy?

JEFF. We're not busy.

DAISY. Serena –

JEFF (*a warning*). Daisy –

DAISY. I know we haven't always seen eye to eye, but for what it's worth, I do feel for you.

SERENA. Since when?

DAISY. I have many yoga students who are going through the same thing, and they bring their suffering to the mat. Why don't I make us all a cup of chai?

She leaves. A beat.

JEFF. Are you okay?

SERENA. I'm great.

JEFF. I've missed you.

SERENA. Looks like it.

SERENA *stares at his crotch – his flies are undone.*
JEFF *zips his fly.*

JEFF. Nothing happened.

SERENA. Bullshit.

A beat.

JEFF. It was just a kiss.

SERENA. Just a kiss.

JEFF. It didn't mean anything.

SERENA. I can't believe I came here.

JEFF. Why did you come here?

SERENA. I came here to ask you if you'd try again.

JEFF. For a baby?

SERENA. A baby. Us. The whole thing. But doesn't matter now, does it? You've moved on.

JEFF. I haven't.

SERENA. Your dick has.

She heads for the door.

JEFF. I'm sorry, okay. I just remembered what it was like to be wanted for my body, not my DNA.

SERENA *stops.*

SERENA. So it's just about the sex?

SERENA *starts tearing her clothes off.*

JEFF. What are you doing?

SERENA. You want a fuck? Let's fuck.

JEFF What, now?

SERENA. Why not?

JEFF. Daisy's coming back.

SERENA. So? Let her watch. Invite the fucking neighbours. I've had people staring up my crack for years.

She grabs at JEFF's *clothes. He resists.*

JEFF. Stop it.

SERENA. Why? You scared of me now?

JEFF. No.

SERENA. Then take out your cock and prove it!

DAISY *enters with a tray of tea on this line.* JEFF *pushes* SERENA *away.*

DAISY. Oh dear. Serena, I have a friend called Rowan, she's a healer and a therapist –

SERENA. Stay out of this, yogini.

DAISY. I know you're having a very hard time right now, but like it or not, Jeff and I have a history.

SERENA. A history of colonial exploitation. You made sure you planted your pussy flag in Africa.

JEFF. Serena!

DAISY. I'm sorry but I won't be spoken to like that in my own house.

SERENA. We live in a one-bedroom flat because twenty years ago you snared him with your fake Hindu *chut*.

DAISY. You probably don't want to hear this now, but having a baby is not the be all and end all –

SERENA. Finish that sentence, you self-entitled bitch and I will rip out your hair by its badly dyed roots and stuff it up your cracker-dry axe wound!

DAISY *exits*.

JEFF. What the hell's wrong with you?

SERENA. Nothing. I just got woke.

JEFF. About what?

SERENA. About us. But I will take the sperm.

JEFF. What?

SERENA. You don't have to be involved. I'll have the baby by myself.

JEFF. You want me to be a sperm donor now?

SERENA. You owe me now, Jeff. You and her.

JEFF. I fucked up, I'm sorry. But I love you.

SERENA. I can forgive you for having a past. And for having Zara. What I can't forgive you for is conceiving her so carelessly with someone you never really loved. And then telling me that *my* desires to be a mother don't count because they're not rational.

She goes to the door. JEFF *grabs and holds her. For a moment, she lets him.*

JEFF. I want to come home. Please.

SERENA *pulls herself away with effort.*

SERENA. You can't. Not now.

Offstage: the sound of school boys singing 'Ave Maria'.

Scene Five

Same night. Music room. After the concert. MILES *removes his tie.*

MILES. I reckon I'm safe for another academic year.

BRIDGET. They loved you. Well done, babe.

They hug. It goes on a little too long. MILES *separates.*

MILES. I was standing there watching those boys sing. They're so confident. All those bright futures, you know?

BRIDGET. Yeah.

MILES. I can imagine you having a son like that. Clear-skinned. Good at maths but plays the oboe. He makes Valentines for his bilingual nannies but supports a consistently Premier League football team.

BRIDGET. He sounds lovely.

MILES. Yeah. But he's not me.

BRIDGET. What? Kind, clever, funny?

MILES. I thought I'd grow up to be the next Rufus Wainwright. Not a low-income homo with terrible taste in men.

BRIDGET. None of that matters, not if you can give a kid love and attention.

MILES. It matters to me. It took me years to come to terms with my failures. But having all my weaknesses manifest in your child, seeing the disappointment in your eyes, and his.

BRIDGET. Miles –

MILES. I know you, Bridget. We could never be equal partners in this. You're too good a businesswoman.

BRIDGET. So you'll pass up the opportunity to be loved unconditionally? Just because it's on my dollar?

MILES. How is that unconditional? I love you. I hope you have the perfect kid with the perfect sperm. But I don't want to be part of the staff.

BRIDGET puts her bag down on the baby monitor, unmuting it. A brief whine of feedback. During the next, their conversation is amplified through the baby monitor.

BRIDGET. I was in love with you once.

MILES. I know.

BRIDGET. I mean really in love, for the first time. Perhaps the only time.

MILES. We were twenty, we didn't know each other's middle names.

BRIDGET. You broke my heart, you wanker.

MILES. Oh, come on. We went to bed twice. I was still in the closet.

BRIDGET. And when you came out? Who took you to Pride for the first time? Got your subscription to *Attitude*? I even bought your condoms.

MILES. You knew my size.

BRIDGET. *That's* unconditional love, babe. I was your parachute when you hurtled down the big gay rabbit hole. You might still be poor, but at least you've got a tribe. I'm on my own. Nobody's judged more in this world than a childless career woman. And you're partly responsible.

MILES. How?

BRIDGET. I got pregnant with your baby. Our baby.

MILES. What?

BRIDGET. It was just before you came out. I was already eight weeks when I found out.

MILES. And you didn't think to tell me?

BRIDGET. You were in love with tiny-dick Daniel. What was I supposed to do?

MILES. So what did you do?

BRIDGET. I got rid of it, Miles.

FATHER SCALES rushes in. He takes BRIDGET*'s bag off the baby monitor and speaks into it.*

FATHER SCALES. 'To all that repent the Lord grants forgiveness.' And for the thirsty, there's fruit punch in reception. See you after the break.

He switches the baby monitor off; the feedback stops.

Lights down.

Interval.

ACT THREE

Scene One

SURTITLE: 'The plains of Mamre, 2000 BC.' We hear a holy choir singing.

CHOIR. Ave Serena, full of grace
Serena, full of grace
Serena, full of grace
Ave, ave
The Lord is with thee

> SARAH (SERENA), *a very old woman, weeps outside her tent. A servant* (MITA) *sweeps up in the background.* ABRAHAM (JEFF), *a very old man, comes out of the tent.*

ABRAHAM. Sarah, my wife. Why do you weep?

SARAH. Do you really have to ask?

ABRAHAM. No. You weep for sorrow that we have not been blessed with a child. But did the Lord not tell you to pray and be patient?

SARAH. It's been seventy years, Abraham. I've worn out a dozen prayer mats. I even let you beget a son with my slave Hagar, the ungrateful bitch, and still my womb stays empty.

ABRAHAM. Your gesture was magnanimous.

SARAH. And now she flaunts her child in front of me. There's gratitude.

> HAGAR (DAISY) *enters – a young attractive Egyptian woman, with her son* ISHMAEL, *fourteen.*

ABRAHAM. Talk of the devil. Greetings, Hagar. Ishmael, my son.

ISHMAEL. Whassup.

ABRAHAM. What is up?

HAGAR. See how he grows, Abe. He looks more like you every day.

ISHMAEL. I'm half-Egyptian, man. Don't box me in.

SARAH *stifles a sob.*

HAGAR. What's wrong with you? Is it your rheumatism again?

SARAH. See how she deliberately torments me?

HAGAR. She's just jealous of my potency. Childless psychotic old hag.

ABRAHAM. Enough! Do I need to remind you both of my authority?

ISHMAEL. You need more than that, bruv, you need a miracle.

Three holy MESSENGERS *appear, disguised as travellers. The first is* MARSHALL, *the second* BRIDGET, *the third* SHARON.

ABRAHAM. Greetings, strangers. Seek you shade from the midday sun?

MESSENGER 1. Yes, good brother. We are on our way to Sodom.

ABRAHAM. Ah, Sodom. A most entertaining city.

MESSENGER 3. But tell us, why are there tears on this old hag's face?

MESSENGER 2. Perhaps we can help her to smile again.

SARAH. Nobody can help. The Lord has abandoned me.

Lights change. The MESSENGERS *shed their cloaks and reveal themselves. The four humans cower.* ABRAHAM *has also transformed – he's now being played by* MILES.

MESSENGER 1. Fear not, family of Abraham. We are divine messengers and bring good tidings.

MESSENGER 2. Sarah will soon conceive her longed-for child and bring your family into profit again.

SARAH *laughs.*

MESSENGER 3. Did you just laugh?

SARAH. No.

MESSENGER 3. You did, I heard you.

SARAH. The whole thing just sounds a bit unrealistic. We're bankrupt. I've had my menopause. Abraham's ninety-nine.

MESSENGER 1. Nobody is too old to be a broker of the bonds of G-D.

ISHMAEL. G-D?

MESSENGER 3. Yes. Adonia.

MESSENGER 2. HaShem.

MESSENGER 1. G-D.

ISHMAEL. What happened to the O?

MESSENGER 3. He is too holy and too terrible for an O.

ISHMAEL. Oh.

ABRAHAM. Forgive my son's curious mind. He is a student of Anthropology, with my full support.

SARAH. Abraham? You've changed.

MESSENGER 1. Hark, Sarah, hark. You will bear a son and call him Isaac.

SARAH *celebrates with* ABRAHAM.

MESSENGER 2. In time the prophet Jesus will be born to Isaac's tribe, and great works shall be done in his name.

ISHMAEL. What about the Crusades?

HAGAR. Well done, darling.

MESSENGER 3. We are holy messengers and as such we have no sociopolitical agenda.

MESSENGER 1. Isaac will bear sons who will bear sons who will bear sons until the Jewish nation has descendants as numerous as the stars.

HAGAR. What about my son? You can't disinherit him just because he's half-Egyptian.

MESSENGER 1. Do not despair. Ishmael will have twelve sons of his own.

MESSENGER 2. His line will beget the prophet Mohammed, thus fathering the Arab nation.

ABRAHAM. So the Arab and Israeli nations will be born out of sibling rivalry? That sounds potentially divisive.

MESSENGER 3. We foresee no long-term situation.

The SERVANT *speaks up. She has an Indian accent.*

SERVANT. Now I've heard it all.

MESSENGER 1. Silence, slave! G-D is a generous benefactor.

MESSENGER 3. He's CEO of the cosmos, mate.

SERVANT. So what? (*To* SARAH.) Don't waste your time on all these male seed-bearers with their pointless foreskins.

MESSENGER 2. This is sacrilege. *We* will not waste our time on nonbelievers.

The MESSENGERS *depart, taking* ABRAHAM, HAGAR *and* ISHMAEL *with them.*

SARAH. Don't go! (*To the* SERVANT.) They just promised me a baby.

SERVANT. Promises, promises. It's no wonder women believe they have no power.

The SERVANT *leads* SARAH *to a bed.*

SARAH. Who are you?

SERVANT. Keep up. I am the mother goddess, Shakti, the divine female.

SARAH. Last time you were my vagina. And why the broom?

SERVANT. I'm here to sweep away the old system. No more fantasies. It's time for action.

She forces SARAH *to lie down, singing an Indian lullaby.*
SARAH *falls asleep. The servant takes off her robe,*
revealing a sari. She is MITA, *sixties. They are in*
SERENA*'s bedroom.*

MITA *continues to sing the lullaby –* SERENA *mutters to*
herself, tossing and turning. She wakes up and throws off the
covers. She's in a ratty dressing gown, with unwashed hair.

MITA. Bad dream?

SERENA. It was good till you turned up.

MITA. Sit up.

SERENA. I'm tired.

MITA. You're tired because you're always lying down. Up!

She pulls SERENA *up into a sitting position.* SERENA
removes an empty ice-cream tub from the bedclothes. She
tosses it on the floor and reaches for a bag of crisps.

And enough junk, you've been farting like a goat.

She takes the crisps away from SERENA.

SERENA. I'm hungry.

MITA *brings out a mango and slices it.*

MITA. Here, your favourite. Now tell me about this dream. I'll
interpret it for you.

SERENA (*closing her eyes, remembering*). They told me I'd
have a son… it was God's will.

MITA. Who was the father?

SERENA. Jeff… I think.

MITA. Have you spoken to Jeff recently?

SERENA. Not since he moved in with Brendan.

MITA. You still haven't forgiven him.

SERENA. He cheated on me.

MITA. And you'll punish him forever for a single moment of
madness?

SERENA. Whose side are you on?

MITA. Always these 'sides'. You're such an Englishwoman.

MITA *gives* SERENA *the mango.*

SERENA. I don't want it. And you chose to have me here.

MITA. I didn't want you to have the same struggles I'd had in India.

SERENA. I'm struggling to get pregnant, aren't I?

MITA. Lying in your own dirt for weeks on end won't help you there.

SERENA (*losing it*). Have you ever tried to get your hands on decent fresh sperm? There's a thousand men on Facebook prepared to come round and masturbate in my bathroom, but not a single one I'd share a mango with.

SERENA *eats the mango.* MITA *opens* SERENA*'s laptop.*

MITA. I've had a look at the donor pages. Some of them seem like reasonable men.

SERENA. Yeah? Show me one.

MITA. Paul here has completed seventeen mara*thans*?

SERENA. He's also fifty-one and can't spell.

MITA. Okay what about this one?

SERENA. Jordan, twenty-one. Looking to co-parent. Donation type 'to be discussed'. Which means he's after natural insemination.

MITA. Intercourse? And would you consider that?

SERENA. No! I'm not having sex with a stranger. Especially not with you in the same bed.

MITA. And you're sure we cannot buy some seed from a reputable salesman with no strings attached?

SERENA. You're not allowed to sell it, Mum.

MITA. I'm just trying to find solutions. You were never a practical child.

MITA *gets into the bed.*

SERENA. What are you doing?

MITA. If you won't get out I'll get in. Which side is mine?

SERENA (*pointing*). The sofa-bed side, next door.

MITA. What is the problem? We shared a bed until you were nine years old.

SERENA. And you wonder why Dad left.

MITA. He left because I kicked him out. All these father figures you invest in like this famous doctor are just mortal men, not gods.

SERENA *gets out of bed and snatches up a pillow and a blanket.*

Where are you going?

SERENA. I'll sleep on the sofa.

MITA. I'm just trying to help you. And look, I got you out of bed at last. Now, here is how I learned to survive in this country. If rules must be followed, first you must find out what they are, and then you must find out how to bend them.

Scene Two

Same day. MILES *in an 'Assisted Ownership' office with a young* SALES ADVISER. *He taps on a laptop.*

ADVISER. So, to recap, Mr Fisher.

MILES. Call me Miles.

ADVISER. To recap, Miles, you're a single man in full-time employment – a music teacher at St Brice's Catholic School for Boys.

MILES. Erm…

ADVISER. I went to a Catholic school myself. What it lacked in laughs it made up for in woodworking. Children?

MILES. No.

ADVISER. That'll help. Right, let's input the data and see what comes up. (*Consulting laptop*.) So you are... a category F.

MILES. Is that good?

ADVISER. I'm not sure, I'm still in training. We're told to leave the judgement to the market. (*Hands over a brochure*.) So. These are the Assisted Ownership properties in your bracket. Do you have any idea of what you're looking for?

MILES. In an ideal world, a Georgian terrace. Period features. No ghosts, no damp, no laminate flooring. Obviously I'm prepared to compromise. (*Flips through the brochure*.) Hounslow. Southall. Knockholt? Is that even in London?

ADVISER. What it is, is Greater London. Well, Kent, really.

MILES. I already live in Zone 4. I can't go out any further.

ADVISER. It's affordable housing. Most people are lucky to get a foot on the property ladder now.

MILES. And the ladder leads to Kent?

ADVISER. My partner lives in Kent. It's only a forty-minute commute door to door.

MILES. I know, my ex-therapist moved there. But, you know. Harvester pubs. Lonely goths smoking at bus stations.

ADVISER. What's a goth?

MILES. These places remind me too much of where I grew up. No theatre, no cinema, just five charity shops and a bar where you got nutted if you knew the words to Smiths songs. Oh. I like this one. One bed, Zone 3, balcony, high-gloss kitchen.

ADVISER. What it is, is you're not eligible for that property. You'd need a yearly income of seventy to ninety K and a much bigger deposit.

MILES. How is that affordable housing?

ADVISER. How about this one? Barratt new build. Zone 5, five-year fittings warranty, share of outdoor space.

MILES. A garden?

ADVISER. There's a shrub centrepiece in the entry courtyard. It's available now. Is your deposit cash ready?

MILES. Yes. Well, I've had to dip into my savings a bit. I had to take some time off work for personal reasons.

ADVISER. So you *aren't* currently in full-time employment?

MILES. I'll be back in a few weeks, hopefully.

ADVISER. It will have a negative impact on your credit scoring.

MILES. Please. Look, I know I've made mistakes in the past. The Conran Shop store card. Music and Anthropology. But I'm a good man. I teach children to sing Beatles songs for a living. I just need a break.

ADVISER. What it is, is… I like you, Miles. At least you're honest. So between us. If you can find a way to match your monthly salary for a period of twelve weeks, I can clear your record and we'll start again.

MILES. Where the hell am I going to find that sort of money?

ADVISER. I don't know, mate. Have you got something you can sell?

Elsewhere BRIDGET *appears, on her phone, leaving a message.*

BRIDGET. It's me. Again. Christ, you like playing hard-to-get, don't you, babe? Look, I said I was sorry, I said it was bad timing, I said I didn't mean to make Bono cry. Are you going to sulk for another two months or are you going to grow up and call me back? I'm fine, by the way, thanks for asking.

Scene Three

Clinic waiting room, a few days later. SERENA *sits.* KIKI *is on the phone.*

KIKI. I'm afraid he's exceptionally busy right now. You're welcome to drop in and pick up an information pack on pre-conception body optimisation. Yes, it is a completely free leaflet. Thank you. (*Hangs up. To* SERENA.) Sorry about that. How can I help?

SERENA. Is Dr Marshall available today?

KIKI. Today? You're looking at a six-week wait, I'm afraid he's exceptionally busy right now.

SERENA. Not even for a five-minute chat?

KIKI. That would be a complimentary mini-consultation. Is it in reference to ongoing treatment?

SERENA. No.

KIKI. In that case I'd need to book you in for a full consultation-stroke-former-treatment-pathway review. That's not mini. Or complimentary. Can I ask what it's regarding?

SERENA. It's regarding sperm donors.

KIKI. I can give you our list of recommended Cryobanks.

SERENA. I need live sperm, not frozen. The doctor thinks my chances are better that way.

KIKI. A known donor, then. Do you have someone in mind? A family friend, perhaps?

SERENA. That's right. But I'd like to know more about the legal implications before I go ahead.

MILES *comes out of the consulting room, whistling, with a slip of paper. He takes a seat.*

KIKI. Once his sperm's been quarantined, as long as he signs the necessary paperwork in a licensed clinic, which we are, obviously, he won't be liable for financial support or have any paternal rights. Unless that's what you decide you want.

MILES *pretends not to listen.* SERENA *goes to the desk and lowers her voice.*

SERENA. Does the quarantine take long?

KIKI. We can fast-track him, if he's a *very* well-known donor and there's a medical history available. (*Glances at* MILES.) Would you mind if I deal with this gentleman quickly?

SERENA. Sure.

She sits down. MILES *goes to the desk.*

MILES. How much do I owe you?

KIKI. Full follow-up consultation on your comprehensive semen MOT... that's two hundred and sixty-five pounds please.

MILES. I was only in there ten minutes.

KIKI. Dr Marshall doesn't charge by the minute, sir.

MILES *hands over his debit card.*

KIKI. Did I mention we've got an offer on our relaxation and nutrition pack?

MILES. Oh, no thanks –

KIKI. It includes aromatherapy candles, protein bars, and two months' supply of our pre-conception supplement to help prevent oxidative damage to the sperm.

MILES. I don't need it.

KIKI. Oh?

MILES (*waving his slip of paper*). The Usain Bolt of semen. Volume, motility. It's got wings.

He puts in his PIN – the machine beeps, it's out of paper.

KIKI. Sorry, the paper's run out. It's our busiest time. Back-to-school, Harvest Festival – difficult for our clients. Won't be a sec.

She goes into the back. MILES *sits down and smiles at* SERENA. *He hums 'Ave Maria'.*

SERENA *tries not to stare at him.*

MILES. Lovely day.

SERENA. What?

MILES. Nothing, just… it's a lovely day. Golden. Crisp. Makes me want to buy new school shoes.

SERENA. Have we met before?

MILES. I don't think so.

SERENA. Good news, is it? I overheard.

MILES. Yes, good news.

SERENA. That should please your partner.

MILES. I don't have a partner. Though with a sperm count like this I might not be single for long.

SERENA. Why have the tests then?

MILES. Oh, you know. Self-evaluation. Assessing the old stocks and shares in case…

SERENA. You're going to donate?

MILES. Perhaps. We don't get paid, of course. It's outrageous really, considering how much the banks sell it on for.

SERENA. I'd gladly pay a good donor. I mean, if I knew what I was getting.

MILES. It does happen apparently.

SERENA. Really?

MILES. Yeah. Jam jars being handed over in car parks for envelopes of cash.

SERENA. How much cash?

MILES. I've no idea. It's risky, though.

SERENA. Very risky. Although…

MILES. What?

SERENA. Well… I suppose it depends how much the woman needs the sample and the man needs the money.

KIKI *comes back in and prints out* MILES*'s receipt.*

KIKI. There you go, sir. Anything else we can do for you?

MILES. I don't think so, thanks.

KIKI (*to* SERENA). Did you want to book that appointment? I've got an opening in mid-November.

    MILES *and* SERENA *exchange a look.*

MILES. Cup of coffee?

SERENA. Why not. (*To* KIKI.) I've just run into an old –

MILES. Very old friend.

SERENA. Friend of the family.

MILES (*overlapping*). Of the family.

Scene Four

A few days later. SERENA*'s living room.* MILES *sits on the sofa between* MITA *and* SERENA.

SERENA. Miles is a music teacher. In a very good Catholic boys school.

MITA. You're a Catholic? I'm surprised.

MILES. I'm not Catholic myself. More of a pan-agnostic. I'm not sure God exists but if he does he's probably not a man with a beard but a twelve-year-old Chinese girl. I like to practise all-inclusive spiritual doubt.

    He laughs, nervous. MITA *doesn't laugh.*

    It's a nice school. I've always loved boys… (*Alarmed*) kids… as students, I mean, their passion – *musical* passion, they're just so alive and full of… beans…

MITA. My daughter tells me you're gay.

MILES. Yes.

MITA. No diseases.

SERENA. Mum!

MILES. It's okay. I've shown Serena my bloods. And my
disclosure and barring certificate.

SERENA. And his family medical history.

MILES. Both parents still alive. Separated and miserable but
with own teeth and hair.

MITA. Have you told your parents of this plan?

MILES. No. I don't think they'd understand.

MITA. I'm not sure I do. But as I am paying for the sample
I thought I had the right to examine the raw materials.

She studies him intently.

MILES. Of course. It'll be your grandchild. I mean if we
manage to...

SERENA. Put down a big enough deposit.

MILES *and* SERENA *laugh a bit too loudly.* MITA *doesn't
laugh. They stop.*

MILES. Sorry. This is all a bit...

SERENA. Surreal.

MITA. The curse of my generation is that we were only taught
how to look after men and children. Yours is that you only
know how to look after yourselves and you can't even do
that right. Too much choice, that's the problem. Gay, straight,
crooked –

SERENA. Mum –

MITA. Man, woman, animal, mineral – it's no wonder so many
of you can't have children. How would a new soul even
know where to attach itself?

SERENA. It's going to work this time. I can feel it.

MILES. I can feel it too.

MITA. There's a lot of feeling going on and not much thinking. Have you discussed how you'll manage the legalities?

MILES (*takes out a piece of paper*). I spoke to the lawyer. I won't be named as the legal father if I sign the Genesis donor forms. But we should draw up a contact between us anyway spelling out our personal arrangement.

SERENA (*of the paper*). Is that it?

MILES. Yes. I got it from the Which? website.

MITA. Then what?

SERENA. Then we go back to the clinic, we pretend he's a known donor.

MILES. A friend of the family.

SERENA. My piano teacher.

MILES. Yes! I'm giving you lessons. Private tuition, exclusive rates.

MITA. Piano lessons have gone up since I was a girl.

MILES. I'm a good teacher. And Serena is desperate to learn.

MITA. In my experience, Mr Fisher –

MILES. Miles.

MITA. In my experience, Miles Fisher, desperation does one of two things. It makes you resourceful or it makes you very, very stupid. I know which my daughter is. My question is, which one are you?

MILES. To be honest, Mrs Goswami… I'm still figuring that out.

MITA *finally smiles*.

MITA. Good. An honest man. This we can work with.

MITA *goes to* MILES *and takes his chin in her hand, gazing into his eyes*.

If the soul is not crooked then I am content. And yours – it is a straight road.

MILES (*moved*). Thank you.

SERENA. Whereas I'm just stupid.

MITA. Serena, *beti*. If you have a baby you will learn that you don't love your child in spite of its weakness. But because of it. I remember the first time I held you. Ugly little scrap, you were. Yellow, like a squinting mango. I thought, what have I done. And then – whoosh.

MILES. Pee?

MITA. Love. I couldn't have stopped it if I'd tried.

MILES. Does it ever dry up?

MITA. Sometimes it gets blocked. But it always comes back. (*Takes the contract from* MILES.) So. I will be your witness to this act of love. Let us proceed.

Scene Five

Surgery. Classical music on the surgery stereo. An EMBRYOLOGIST and a NURSE in surgical scrubs and masks sedate SERENA and lift her legs into stirrups.

EMBRYOLOGIST. Can you change the station, Nurse?

NURSE. What do you fancy, Doctor?

EMBRYOLOGIST. Magic FM? I work better to a beat.

The NURSE changes the station. A classic disco track plays. The EMBRYOLOGIST does a little dance.

NURSE. Ready to go in?

EMBRYOLOGIST. Ready.

The EMBRYOLOGIST disappears between SERENA's legs under the sheet.

Elsewhere a MALE NURSE shows MILES into the comfort suite. Muzak on a speaker.

MALE NURSE. So, welcome to the engine room. I apologise for the music. Not my choice, but the room's not soundproof.

MILES. Good to know.

MALE NURSE. I apologise for the decor, too, or lack thereof. And the magazines. I have asked management for something a little less discriminatory, if you get my drift. But will they listen?

He gives MILES *a sterile plastic jar with a pink lid.*

So, fingers on the outside only, please. Seal it quick as possible and press the buzzer when you're done. Enjoy.

He leaves. MILES *sits on a chair and starts flipping through the porn mags.*

MILES. Tits. Ass. Tits. (*A closer look.*) Ugh.

He closes his eyes, puts his hand down his trousers.
A hoodied TEENAGER *of indeterminate gender appears and sits next to him.* MILES *opens his eyes.*

Oh, please, not now.

TEENAGER. That's not a very warm welcome.

MILES. What am I suppose to say? My, how you've grown?

TEENAGER. Don't be flippant, Dad. You summoned me. Well go on, have a good gander.

MILES. You don't look like me.

TEENAGER. I never had the chance to develop properly.

MILES. You're angry, fair enough. But I didn't know she was pregnant.

TEENAGER. You know now. That's why you're trying to deal with your guilt by fathering a child you'll never see.

MILES. I might end up being involved… birthdays, Christmases…

TEENAGER. Sounds a bit half-baked. Like me. And one baby's not going to buy you a flat in Zone 3.

MILES. I'll set up a website. There must be hundreds of women who'll pay for Grade-A fresh sperm.

TEENAGER. Are you sure you're not doing this to punish Bridget? Because for once there's something you can have that she can't?

MILES. No. Now can I get on with it please?

He turns away and fumbles with himself. BRIDGET *appears, as her student self. Massive hair, hoop earrings, early nineties knock-off designer garms.*

BRIDGET. Having it would have been the punishment.

MILES. Oh, God.

BRIDGET. Look at me. I was twenty. What kind of life could we have given it?

MILES. There's no point asking now, you made the decision for both of us.

BRIDGET. You were a child, babe, you still had acne on your neck and a novelty lunchbox.

MILES. So what? We could have been young platonic hip co-parents... like David and Angie Bowie in their glam bicurious phase. Oh, that's working.

He closes his eyes and fumbles again. SUSAN SONTAG *appears.*

SUSAN. So your desire for agency through fatherhood is tied to your sexuality?

MILES. Susan Sontag? Wow. It is such an honour. (*To everyone.*) She wrote the seminal book *AIDS and its Metaphors.*

He puts his hand down his trousers again.

BRIDGET (*to everyone*). He discovered queer politics after the cashmere-washer gave him crabs.

MILES *takes his hand out again.*

SUSAN. Did you hear what you just said, Miles? It's no accident that we use the word 'seminal', with its inherent male potency to describe something of great influence.

MILES. It's a compliment.

SUSAN. If I was still alive I'd have plenty to say about the linguistics of infertility.

TEENAGER. How's that supposed to help him get a stiffy?

BRIDGET. Oh, he loves it, he was always a closet intellectual.

SUSAN. The 'tragic defeminised woman', unable to conceive because of flawed biology or bad life choices.

BRIDGET. Social infertility, they like to call it. As if we chose to wait half our lives to get a decent job for which we're paid less than men.

SUSAN. I haven't finished my analogy.

BRIDGET. No affordable childcare, bugger-all maternity pay and we're the ones who are diseased!

SUSAN. Hence her quest for 'the strong male semen' to vanquish her despair.

MILES. And it'll only go to waste. I've been throwing it away for years.

SUSAN. And now you're using it to vanquish your own lack of sexual and economic power? Becoming a father won't make you feel less poor or less homosexual.

MILES. I don't want to feel less homosexual, I want to feel significant. And I'm on a time limit here.

BRIDGET. You're significant to me. We've had each other's backs for half our lives and now you've thrown me over for a total stranger.

MILES. See, you're still trying control me, even in here.

SUSAN. It's the patriarchal system that controls us, by defining us in relation to what we are *not*. i.e. gays are less than straights, blacks are less than whites.

BRIDGET. Women are less than men.

TEENAGER. And the childless are less than parents, therefore not truly human.

SUSAN. He's smart for his age.

BRIDGET. He? It was a girl.

MILES. How do you know?

TEENAGER. She doesn't. And actually I identify as non-binary.

MILES. Look, you can't talk me out of this one, it's too late now.

BRIDGET. And who are *you* going to talk to when it all goes wrong? You still won't answer my calls.

MILES. Why should I? You got me fired!

SUSAN (*to* TEENAGER). It's probably just as well you went back into the waiting room.

TEENAGER. Yeah. Next time I might get born a pop star or a management consultant.

MILES (*closing his eyes*). Management. José Mourinho. Obama. Sadiq Khan.

He fumbles with himself again. Outside, a knock.

MALE NURSE (*off*). You all right in there, Mr Fisher?

MILES. I'm coming! Almost.

The MALE NURSE enters.

MALE NURSE. Just wanted to check you hadn't fallen in.

He removes his scrubs and becomes FATHER SCALES.

MILES. Brian, thank God.

FATHER SCALES. This is an abomination. No child should be conceived through masturbation assisted by pornography.

MILES. It won't now you're here.

He grabs FATHER SCALES and kisses him.

FATHER SCALES. What are you doing?

MILES. I assumed you had latent homosexual tendencies.

FATHER SCALES. No! Before I started Formation I was engaged to a girl called Desiree but I realised I loved her like a sister. It doesn't mean I'm gay.

MILES. False consciousness, angel. We've all been through it.

FATHER SCALES. Are you sure?

MILES. Oh wow, your self-doubt's making me hard. Quick, Susan.

He gestures at the sperm receptacle – she hands it to him.

SUSAN. Interesting… pink plastic.

MILES *pushes* FATHER SCALES *into the corner cubicle and pulls the curtains.*

A buzzer goes. Segue to SERENA *on the gurney. Disco music on the surgery stereo. The* EMBRYOLOGIST *checks* SERENA *over. She groans and comes round.*

SERENA. Is it over?

EMBRYOLOGIST (*American*). Sure is, honey. We got seven good eggs. Now waiting to be fertilised with that gay honky's power sperm. You gonna have you a real love child.

SERENA. What kind of doctor are you?

The EMBRYOLOGIST *removes his mask and gown, revealing a seventies outfit. He dances to the music.*

EMBRYOLOGIST. Don't worry, girl, you're still high as a kite from the Propofol. I'm just a dream. A *disco* dream.

He helps SERENA *sit up.*

You okay, sweetie?

SERENA. Yeah, it's just this song reminds me of Jeff. It was playing the first time we met. Seventies Night at the Carwash Club.

The EMBRYOLOGIST *becomes* JEFF. *He dances with a team of medics. During the dance we see eggs inseminated with sperm onscreen. The cells start to divide and make two, then three, then four-cell embryos. Two of the embryos die. Three survive.*

KIKI *appears.*

KIKI. Congratulations, Mrs Robertson-Goswami. Five of your seven eggs have successfully fertilised and are maturing into embryos.

JEFF sweeps SERENA into his arms and they dance together.

JEFF. You took the piss out of my moves all night.

SERENA. I was trying to hide how much I liked you.

JEFF. It didn't work.

SERENA. We *were* happy, weren't we?

JEFF. We were the best.

SERENA. Can you be happy for me now? Say it, Jeff.

JEFF. Say what?

SERENA. Say you don't love me any more.

JEFF. I'm not being forced into a corner here.

SERENA. If you want to help me, for God's sake, just say it.

KIKI. Say it.

JEFF. No. Not this time. It isn't true.

Onscreen: two of the embryos die. Three continue to develop until they become blastocysts.

KIKI. Three of your five embryos developed into blastocysts and two are ready to be implanted.

Another SURGEON appears. SERENA is back on the bed, ready for implantation.

WOMB. Welcome to your womb with a view. Come on, you've been waiting for that all night, haven't you?

SURGEON. Can you change the station, please? We want to give these embryos a decent chance.

The NURSE changes the radio station – Schubert's 'Ave Maria' plays. The SURGEON is about to implant the embryos. JEFF appears again.

JEFF. Wait. It's not too late to change your mind.

SERENA. You can't talk me out of this one, Jeff.

JEFF. You'd throw away everything we had for this?

SERENA. I want to create something that's mine.

> SURGEON *takes off her scrubs and becomes an old Indian woman.*

GREAT-GRANDMOTHER. You don't need embryos to do that, dear.

SERENA. Who are you?

GREAT-GRANDMOTHER. I am your great-grandmother. I suffered many miscarriages before I bore my only child. But she was stillborn.

JEFF. How did Serena get here, then?

GREAT-GRANDMOTHER. At the hospital I agreed to nurse an infant whose mother had just died in childbirth. My breasts were full and the poor mite was so hungry. In this way we healed each other's pain.

SERENA. I've heard this story. (*To* JEFF.) She adopted her.

GREAT-GRANDMOTHER. She was my beloved daughter, regardless of her bloodline.

SERENA. That's beautiful.

GREAT-GRANDMOTHER. Your longing is a heavy burden. But it is also divine. Without that urge to love the human river would soon run dry.

SERENA. If it's divine why does it hurt so much?

GREAT-GRANDMOTHER. The greatest love of all is unconditional. Not biological, nor bound by laws of science.

GOD (*off*). Love is so unnecessary now we've deregulated the conception market.

SERENA. Is that who I think it is?

KIKI. It's the Master of the Universe.

JEFF. Oh, Christ.

GREAT-GRANDMOTHER. No, boy, it's G-D.

    GOD *appears in a flash of blue sky.*

GOD. Lovely evening. If I do say so myself.

JEFF. He's still hardwired in your system. Like a virus.

    JEFF *leaves.* KIKI *elbows* GREAT-GRANDMOTHER *out of the way and implants the embryos.* GOD *distracts* SERENA *while* KIKI *does it.*

GOD. Look up at the night sky. What do you see?

SERENA. Stars?

GOD. Stars are dead, my dear. (*Points.*) Ova. Seed. Floating in a Milky Way of nitrous oxide.

SERENA. Are any of them mine?

GOD. Yes. One decent embryo, frozen for future use.

SERENA. Thank God.

GOD. You're very welcome. But you may not need it now. Kiki, presentation.

    KIKI *presents* SERENA *with a pregnancy test stick on a velvet cushion.*

You are ready to be a fully realised member of the human race. Yes, my dear, you are with child.

    SERENA *looks at the pregnancy stick. It glows blue.*

SERENA. It's a miracle.

Scene Six

MARSHALL *onscreen delivering a press statement on Sky News.* BRIDGET *is in her office watching the TV screen. It's three weeks later.*

MARSHALL. Forty years ago a little miracle called Louise Brown was born via IVF. The scientific gains to humankind since then are incalculable. Pre-implantation diagnosis, new flash-freezing methods for preserving eggs – these are just two of our new weapons in the reproductive revolution.

   LARISSA *enters and watches for a moment with her.* BRIDGET *remotes off the sound.*

LARISSA. One of those wind-on-the-face moments, isn't it. When you feel just how far you've come.

BRIDGET. Yeah.

LARISSA. Cheer up, darling. You've been promoted... tomorrow we're going to market.

BRIDGET. I know.

LARISSA. But...

BRIDGET. I'm just wondering if I've done the right thing.

LARISSA. You may not have smashed the glass ceiling but you've headbutted it. Don't start complaining about the migraine.

BRIDGET. Not me. Us. The float.

LARISSA. We're ready for battle, aren't we? There's no news in the market to worry us?

BRIDGET. No, everything's solid. But... did you hear him talking about egg freezing just now?

LARISSA. Yeah. He's a bloody good PR.

BRIDGET. Before I had mine done I asked him how many babies had been born from frozen eggs at Genesis. He said it was probably less than twenty. When we did the clinic audit I got to see his birth records. He didn't lie. It *was* less than twenty. It was zero.

LARISSA. Wow. He's even better at spin than I thought.

BRIDGET. We've gone on record with a live birth rate of zero to twenty per cent. It's on the offer document.

LARISSA. And that's factually correct, right?

BRIDGET. Well, yeah. But is it misleading? I mean, that's not even the worst statistic.

LARISSA. Go on, impress me.

BRIDGET. A woman he was treating had twins by IVF last year. One of the babies only lived three days, but they both went down on his live birth tally. It's completely legal. It just seems…

LARISSA. What? The shareholders won't give a rat's arse about dead babies as long as the figures are alive and kicking.

BRIDGET. Even when the profits come from betting on human failure?

A beat. LARISSA *takes her heels off.*

LARISSA. That's better. Go on, darling. This is between us.

BRIDGET *takes her heels off.*

Are you really wobbling about ethics here? Or is this about the eggs you've got on ice?

BRIDGET. I don't know. Maybe. I suppose I never thought I'd be working out my future in percentages.

LARISSA. What's wrong with that? It all comes down to fractions in the end. You got to calculate what matters so you can make the right decisions.

BRIDGET. It sounds easy when you put it like that.

LARISSA. I wasn't born a motherfucker, you know. Where I grew up most girls had three brats before they were twenty-one. I just wanted to get out there. But that doesn't mean that I don't have regrets.

BRIDGET. You mean not having kids?

LARISSA. Sometimes. But I found something else to love.

BRIDGET. Hugo.

LARISSA. Hugo? Numbers. Numbers don't forget your
anniversary or fuck the help. Every day you take the losses
and then you wake up with a clean slate and fall in love all
over again. But to be a COO you got to put them first. If this
has all got too emotional for you and you can't think straight,
you might spook the float.

BRIDGET. I won't.

LARISSA. You sure? It's not too late to step aside.

BRIDGET. No way. I never show the beast my fear.

She puts her heels back on. LARISSA *follows suit.*

LARISSA. That's my girl. See you at the bell.

She leaves. BRIDGET *slumps. She makes a call on her
mobile.*

BRIDGET. It's me again. I don't know what to say any more.
I just… I need help with my fractions, Miles. And to hear
your voice. Please call me back this time. Please, babe.

Scene Seven

*The stock-market opening bell rings. Next day. Clinic reception.
MARSHALL and KIKI are watching the London Stock
Exchange live on a laptop. MARSHALL is on his mobile phone
talking to BRIDGET. We see her in her office.*

BRIDGET. Are you watching live?

KIKI (*peering at the screen*). It's at four-twenty-three.

MARSHALL. It seems to have slowed off a bit.

BRIDGET. That's normal. It'll pick up in ten minutes when the
foreign markets open.

KIKI. Four-twenty-four.

MARSHALL. Are you sure we didn't go in too low?

BRIDGET. Did you see the feeding frenzy when the bell went this morning?

MARSHALL. We were biting our nails.

BRIDGET. We went in low to create demand and push the share price up. It's basic market logic, Joseph. And it'll happen again.

KIKI. It's stopped.

BRIDGET. Just hold your nerve. I promised you we wouldn't sell your stock for less than five-fifty each. I'll confirm when we hit it –

MARSHALL. If we hit it.

BRIDGET. *When* we hit it.

Another call comes through on her mobile. She checks her phone.

Joseph, I'm going to have to call you back. Check out CNBC for the hourly bulletin.

She switches the other call.

MARSHALL. We've got to hold our nerve. And turn on CNBC.

BRIDGET (*into phone*). Miles. What is it, what's wrong?

BRIDGET *exits.* KIKI *changes the channel. A news report flashes up; 'Stock of the Hour – Genesis Inc.'*

KIKI. Stock of the hour – Genesis Inc.

MARSHALL. We're on television, baby!

They do a little dance. JEFF *and* SHARON *enter.* SHARON *holds her arm carefully.*

We're closed today. We sent an email out.

JEFF. This won't take long.

KIKI. Did you hear the doctor? We're exceptionally busy right now.

SHARON. Watching telly?

KIKI. It's CNBC, actually, we've gone to market.

JEFF *stands by them and watches the screen.*

JEFF. You're selling the company?

MARSHALL. It's a natural growth strategy.

JEFF. Then you can afford to lose one patient.

MARSHALL. If you want a new appointment, talk to Kiki.

JEFF. I don't want an appointment. I want you to stop treating my
    wife. (*Thrusts a letter under* MARSHALL*'s nose.*) I got this in
    the post this morning. A credit agreement between you and
    Serena. Two full cycles repayable over twenty-four months.

MARSHALL. This is a private letter.

JEFF. It was redirected to *me* at my new address.

SHARON. She kicked him out.

KIKI. Are you his mother?

SHARON. He's my caseworker. He's taking me to A&E to
    X-ray my arm.

MARSHALL *hands the letter back to* KIKI.

MARSHALL. It's regrettable. I'll make sure we amend our files.

JEFF. So what, she's going to use a sperm donor? Or has she
    met someone else?

MARSHALL. Mrs Robertson-Goswami is a solo client now
    and I can't discuss her case.

JEFF. Her loan, you mean. At eight per cent.

MARSHALL. She's a woman in great pain who deserves a
    chance to realise her heart's desire.

JEFF. She's an addict! You may as well offer a junkie a dose of
    heroin.

KIKI. It's going up!

MARSHALL *and* KIKI *crowd around the screen.*

MARSHALL. Look, Mr Robertson-Gos... can I call you Jeff? As I understand it, you chose not to have any further treatment.

KIKI. Four-thirty... four-thirty-five...

JEFF. Chose? We couldn't afford it. Seven thousand in your pocket, fifty in the last three years. My car, our pension, our marriage. And what about her sanity?

MARSHALL. I understand it's difficult to quantify the genesis of human life.

JEFF (*overlapping*). Of human life. What is wrong with you people?

SHARON *takes* JEFF *to the sofa and makes him sit down.*

KIKI. Four-fifty-seven, Joseph! Doctor.

The reception phone rings.

(*Into phone.*) Genesis Inc., Kiki speaking, how can I help? Can you talk a little slower?

SHARON. Now you know what it's like trying to get any sense out of Social Services.

KIKI. And how heavy is the bleeding, Mr Fisher?

SHARON. Come on.

JEFF *goes to the reception desk to get the credit agreement letter.*

KIKI. It sounds like nothing to worry about, a bit of spotting is quite normal. Just tell Mrs Robertson-Gos–

JEFF *hears this and looks at* KIKI.

Oh shit. Excuse my language. Just do what they tell you at A&E and please keep us informed. Bye.

JEFF. Has something happened to Serena?

KIKI. It's a private message.

JEFF. I'm her husband.

KIKI. Still?

SHARON. She's good.

KIKI. We have a code red, doctor.

JEFF. She's not already pregnant, is she?

MARSHALL. I'm going to ask you to leave now.

JEFF. What, so you can sell the baby on the stock exchange?

MARSHALL (*bellowing*). What I'm selling is my expertise, my technology and *my risk*. That is the cost of human life these days and it is worth every damn penny!

JEFF. Tell me which hospital, Kiki.

KIKI. What hospital? And I prefer Ms Martin.

SHARON *grabs* KIKI's *notepad and reads it*.

SHARON. Central.

KIKI. That was very aggressive.

SHARON. You should see me when I'm pissed. (*Offers* JEFF *her good arm*.) Come on.

MARSHALL. This is not your battle any more, sir.

SHARON *advances on* MARSHALL. *He backs away*.

SHARON. You going to stop us? Didn't think so. Fucking bourgeoisie.

Scene Eight

Same day. Outside a hospital. SHARON sits on a bench.
Her arm is in a sling. She fumbles with a packet of cigarettes.
Nearby MILES paces, checking his phone.

Throughout the scene we see the Genesis Inc. share price
continue to rise slowly on a screen.

SHARON. Excuse me? Can you help me get a fag out please?

    MILES *comes over and helps her.*

MILES. Ouch. Is it broken?

SHARON. No, but it got a bit bent. Occupational hazard.

MILES. What do you do?

SHARON. I'm married to a cunt.

    JEFF *enters.* MILES *moves away and continues pacing.*

    Find her?

JEFF. She's with the doctor. They won't tell me anything.

SHARON. I don't mind waiting. Nice A&E this. Juice bar.
    Smoker's patio.

JEFF. I thought you'd stopped.

SHARON. I'm down to ten a day. Twelve on high days and
    hospital days.

    A cackle.

JEFF. The problem is I like you, Sharon. When you refuse to
    take care of yourself I take it personally.

SHARON. Stop fussing. I've already got four kids who think
    I'm a disappointment.

JEFF. You're my client, not my mother.

SHARON. You're adopted though, ain't you.

JEFF. What's that got to do with anything?

SHARON. Ron was fostered, you know. You've got the same
    look about you. Like a cat pissing.

JEFF. Sorry?

SHARON. Sort of angry and ashamed at the same time. He thinks it's his fault his mum couldn't look after him.

JEFF. That didn't turn me into a violent man, did it?

SHARON. His type, the fighters, they take it out on other people. Your type, the do-gooders, they find a cause.

JEFF. You think you're my cause?

SHARON. First me, now this doctor. When you're on a crusade you don't have time to think about your own shit, do you.

JEFF. My wife's in hospital because of that fucking doctor. She thinks if she can't have a baby she'll never know what real love is. It wasn't love I felt the first time I held my daughter. It was fear. This tiny little creature, her life literally in my hands. And I couldn't stop thinking…

SHARON. What?

JEFF. Some woman felt the same way about me once… and then handed me over to strangers.

He chokes up. MILES *pretends not to watch.*

SHARON. Come here.

She hugs him. He resists.

JEFF. I don't know if this is really allowed.

SHARON. Who cares?

JEFF *submits to the hug… then gets lost in it.*

Look at us. We're a right pair, aren't we.

JEFF. None of us choose how we get born and raised. But you can choose to believe you're a valuable human being.

SHARON. I told Ron no more deals, like you said. (*Lifts her arm.*) Look what happened. If I kick him out I'm the one who gets punished. Me and the kids.

JEFF. Not if you let me help you do it. That's my job, Sharon.

SHARON. All right. I'll deal with my shit if you deal with yours.

JEFF. Deal.

MITA *and* SERENA *enter.*

Serena!

MILES. Serena!

JEFF. I've been asking for you –

MILES. – they wouldn't give me any information.

JEFF *and* MILES *look at each other, puzzled.*

JEFF. Who are you?

MILES. I'm Miles. I'm a...

SERENA. An old friend.

MITA (*to* MILES). You didn't need to come. It was a panic over nothing.

MILES. No, I'm glad you called. I assume you're –

SHARON. Jeff.

JEFF. What the hell's going on? Mita?

BRIDGET *enters with a* SECURITY GUARD.

GUARD. This is the patio area, madam. Busy as always.

BRIDGET. He's here. Thanks.

GUARD. No worries.

MILES. Bridget.

BRIDGET. I've been looking for you everywhere.

MILES. I'm glad you found me.

BRIDGET*'s phone rings. She mutes the call.*

BRIDGET. What is it, what's happened? Who are they?

SHARON *waves from the bench.*

SHARON. Sharon. Can someone help me with my fag?

BRIDGET's *phone rings again.*

BRIDGET (*to* MILES). Can you give me a minute?

She checks the phone, then mutes the call. The guard helps SHARON *with her cigarette.* JEFF *goes to* SERENA.

JEFF. You're not going to look at me? Serena? Serena!

SERENA *can't face him.* JEFF *puts a hand on her shoulder.*

GUARD. Invading her personal space won't help, sir. Better to talk it through with a trained mediator.

JEFF. I am a trained mediator. So mind your own fucking business.

GUARD. Okay. But you should know I'm doing a course in family counselling skills so that insult bounced right off me, sir.

SERENA. I'm pregnant.

JEFF. Congratulations.

SERENA. Don't make this harder for me.

JEFF. Harder for *you*?

SERENA. You gave me no choice, Jeff.

BRIDGET (*to* MILES). Sorry… what's this got to do with you?

MILES. The baby's mine.

SERENA. He's my sperm donor.

BRIDGET. Wait… so you refused to help me but you'll donate to a stranger?

MITA. Donate? We paid a thousand pounds for his seed.

JEFF/BRIDGET. What?

MILES (*to* BRIDGET). Your business partner did the IVF.

BRIDGET. You went to Genesis?!

BRIDGET's *phone rings, she mutes the call.*

JEFF. Marshall's your partner. Of course he is.

BRIDGET. Excuse me?

SHARON. He's having a hard time right now.

BRIDGET. Yeah? So am I. (*To* MILES.) I'm your best mate!

GUARD. Wow. This is a very complex relationship knot.

MILES. I exercised my right to choose just like you did twenty years ago.

GUARD. I don't want to interfere but I sense a history of emotional codependence.

BRIDGET. There is no 'co'. I've supported him for half his life.

MILES. That's why I'm trying to do something for myself.

GUARD. If I can ask you –

SHARON. Miles.

GUARD. Miles, did you receive much positive reinforcement from your parents as a child?

MILES. No, I felt like a disappointment to them.

GUARD. And perhaps you looked for validation in your friendship with, er –

SHARON. Bridget.

GUARD. Right, but you felt compromised by the economic power she held over you.

MILES. Exactly.

GUARD. So, Bridget, it may be that this 'deal' has enabled Miles to feel that he's participating in an equal exchange.

MITA. That's very impressive.

GUARD. Behaviour-oriented therapy is a great foundation but I'm moving towards Gestalt.

BRIDGET'*s phone rings*.

JEFF (*to* SERENA). So that's it then. End of story.

SERENA. It's the beginning of it, if I'm lucky.

MILES (*to* BRIDGET). Can you turn that off for once.

BRIDGET *takes the call.*

Oh my God.

BRIDGET (*into phone*). Hello? It's up to you but I'd hold, it seems like the market's still hungry. I'll have to call you back.

She hangs up.

JEFF. Do you people actually know the market's not a real person? The market's hungry, the market's volatile, the market needs an aspirin and a little lie-down –

BRIDGET. Oh do fuck off.

JEFF. Was that the market on the phone? Or was it your pimp Dr Money calling his whore?

Gasps from everyone.

GUARD. Jeff… that use of the H-word felt very hostile although I'm sure you felt a deep sense of provocation.

JEFF. You don't have a clue what I'm feeling.

GUARD. Is it possible that you're projecting your anger on to Bridget when you're actually angry at your wife?

JEFF. I am not angry at my fucking wife!

GUARD. Good, Jeff. Stay in your reality and express that to her directly.

JEFF (*to* SERENA). My reality is we're still married. You didn't think to talk to me before you did this?

SERENA. I knew what you'd say. 'You're mad, you're irrational…'

JEFF. Are these the actions of a reasonable person?

MITA *tries to get between them.*

MITA. Calm down, both of you. The doctor said she had to rest.

SERENA. Can you stay out of this, Mum.

MITA. It's a bit late for that.

SHARON. Let them get on with it, love.

MITA *sits next to* SHARON *and shares her fag.*

SERENA. I want to love something *beyond* reason, do you still not get it?

JEFF. And that's going to make you a good mother? (*To* MILES.) Did she tell you she talks to her pussy?

SERENA. Better than talking to a cock. (*Of* MILES.) He understands what I need.

BRIDGET. He understands a thousand pounds.

MILES (*to* SERENA). Sorry, she can only think in financial terms.

BRIDGET. And you're doing this for love?

MILES. What do you know about love? You only want a baby so you don't end up dying alone in your massive empty penthouse.

BRIDGET. You only want one because you've realised your sperm's the only valuable thing you've got.

GUARD. Everyone, it's okay to express extreme emotions here as long as we all agree it's a safe space.

Conversations start to overlap.

MILES. I wouldn't sell it to you if you were the last woman on earth.

BRIDGET. You think I still want it?

MILES. I think you're angry because I never loved you in the way you wanted.

JEFF (*of* MILES). He's worth a grand, is he?

SERENA. Still counting the pennies, even now.

JEFF. I spent everything I had on us.

SERENA. Apart from Zara's guilt-fund that makes you feel like a less shit dad.

JEFF. That's very maternal of you.

BRIDGET (*to* MILES). I gave up a baby for you.

MILES. You did it for *you*, like everything you do.

BRIDGET. You wanker.

SERENA (*to* JEFF). Well thank God it's not yours!

SHARON (*to the* GUARD). Don't give up your day job, love.

GUARD. I'm only halfway through the course, we haven't done much group work yet.

A patch of blood appears on SERENA*'s crotch. Elsewhere we see the Genesis share price hit its peak.*

MITA. Serena, you're bleeding.

SERENA. No.

BRIDGET. Someone get help.

The GUARD *and* SHARON *exit.* BRIDGET, JEFF *and* MITA *sit* SERENA *down.*

SERENA. Please. Somebody make it stop.

The bell rings for the end of the trading day. Elsewhere we see MARSHALL *and* KIKI *celebrate.*

The scene dissolves… we segue to BRIDGET*'s living room.* MILES, SERENA *and* BRIDGET *sit together.* BRIDGET *reads the paper.* Woman's Hour *on the radio.*

JENNI MURRAY. All that remains is for us to say goodbye. Now we've successfully reversed gender bias in broadcasting we're off air for the foreseeable future. Hmph!

SERENA switches the radio off. BRIDGET *puts down the paper.*

BRIDGET. Another fall in interest rates. Our mortgage is going to go down again.

MILES. Great. We can put the surplus away for childcare.

SERENA. We don't need it. There's a free crèche at Jeff's office now. Why don't we upgrade the piano instead?

MILES. No need. Brian's given me a new organ.

FATHER SCALES *enters.*

FATHER SCALES. In exchange for lessons.

MILES *and* FATHER SCALES *kiss.*

MILES. He's a very fast learner.

JEFF *enters carrying a baby.*

JEFF. Nine hours straight through. We've got the best baby in the world.

The baby gets passed around.

BRIDGET. Either that or it's a robot.

MILES. Our child is not an 'it'.

BRIDGET. I thought we'd decided gender was a construct?

SERENA. I think we should leave it up to her.

MILES. Him.

JEFF. They.

They laugh.

SERENA. I'm starting to see Jeff in her.

JEFF *(kisses her)*. I'm starting to see you.

MILES. I can only see myself. He looks anxious all the time.

BRIDGET. Don't worry. My eggs, my balls.

MARX enters wearing a pinny, carrying a basket of laundry. He addresses the audience as he folds baby clothes.

MARX. So, Utopia. The religious called it Paradise. The Russian peasants saw it as a cow with an infinite supply of milk, as long as everyone took only what they needed. As for you workers of this weary, pixelated century? You call it parenthood.

JEFF takes the baby from SERENA and begins to breastfeed it. SHARON enters with MITA.

SHARON. Right, me and Mita are off to nursery. We're teaching the under-fives about children's rights.

MITA. Everyone, there's baby lasagne for lunch.

SHARON. What, with real baby?

Everyone laughs. DAISY *enters. She is pregnant.*

DAISY. Group yoga in the family room in ten.

BRIDGET. Anyone want to share my mat?

FATHER SCALES *rubs* DAISY*'s belly.*

FATHER SCALES. Anyone want to share my erection?

Everyone laughs again. The baby whimpers. JEFF
breastfeeds it.

MARX (*out*). Look, I'm trying my best here. But children are
the hardest theoretical material – they cannot be owned, nor
abolished.

*The baby cries louder. The group try to soothe it but it
doesn't work. They start to fight over it. The baby unravels
and turns into a blanket.*

Except... if the product cannot be owned, perhaps its
absence can. Every age of revolution comes with great
human loss. So collectivise your loss. Yes. For in this
unequal world, inequality might be the only human currency
that unites us all.

MITA (*to* MARX). That's all very interesting, but enough
talking now. We have work to do.

MARX *removes his beard and becomes part of the actors'
ensemble. Together the actors dismantle the scene and set up
the new one, while* MILES *goes to the piano and plays an
instrumental version of 'The Song of Us'.*

Over this we see LARISSA *leaving a voicemail on*
BRIDGET*'s answerphone.*

LARISSA. Bridget? You walked away from a beautiful sea of
green, girl. Fifty-two million drops of water. I guess you just
didn't want to get wet, eh, darling. Enjoy your gardening
leave.

MITA *takes* SERENA *to a bench outside her school. She gives her a packed lunch and sits with her.*

MITA. Eat, *beti*.

SERENA *eats.* JEFF *enters. He and* SERENA *look at each other – this is a surprise.*

Ah. Good, you came.

SERENA. Mum?

JEFF (*to* SERENA). She asked me to meet her here.

MITA. I did. And now I can go. 'Love always finds an outlet, as a river finds the sea.' This is something my grandmother used to say. Why waste all this good water?

She exits. JEFF *hesitates, then sits down next to* SERENA.

Scene Nine

SERENA *and* JEFF *stay on the bench. Kids shriek joyously in the playground behind them.*

Elsewhere BRIDGET *and* MILES *are in* BRIDGET*'s flat.*

JEFF. Are you sure you're ready to be back to work?

SERENA. I missed my Drama girls.

JEFF. Did they miss you?

SERENA. I think Chantal did, the ADD one. They get attached.

JEFF. Yeah.

SERENA. She asked me if I'd left to have a baby.

JEFF. What did you tell her?

SERENA. The truth. That I'd tried to but it hadn't worked. Back to square one.

JEFF. It's not quite square one. You've got embryos in the bank.

SERENA. One embryo. Not yours.

JEFF. Then we're even, aren't we?

SERENA. You've got Zara, Jeff. We'll never be even.

Segue to MILES *and* BRIDGET.

BRIDGET. How's the flat hunt going?

MILES. On hold. How's the jizz hunt going?

BRIDGET. Same.

MILES. Oh?

BRIDGET. Time out. To think about what I really want. Which is fucking complicated.

MILES. Tell me about it.

BRIDGET. You shouldn't leave it too long. The housing market won't slow down, whatever they tell you.

MILES. Why is it so important that I own where I live? Because the world says I'm not a grown-up until I do?

BRIDGET. It's a pension, babe. You won't get a return investing in anything else.

MILES. Who cares about a return? Renting's fine for now. It's what I can afford.

JEFF and SERENA.

JEFF. You know I still want to be a father with you.

SERENA. After all this?

JEFF. I don't really care how. Our own kid. A frozen one. Even a second-hand one.

A beat.

SERENA. Second-hand?

JEFF. Adopted.

SERENA. I don't think of you as second-hand.

JEFF. What, not worn-out and unwanted?

SERENA. I wanted you.

JEFF. You did once, yeah.

SERENA. I mean, we chose each other, didn't we? In spite of all our flaws. Whereas biology's more...

JEFF. Cruel.

SERENA. Random.

BRIDGET *and* MILES.

MILES. I don't need my own piano either.

BRIDGET. You can always borrow mine.

MILES. Thanks, angel. I've written you a song.

He goes to the piano.

BRIDGET. You know I only ever wanted you to have the best of me, Miles. That's all it's ever been.

MILES. I have had it. Best friend. Best financial adviser. Best mother. We can be a family, can't we, with or without the baby?

BRIDGET. Talk me through it.

MILES *plays the song intro. Segue to* SERENA *and* JEFF.

SERENA. Biology's just desperate to replicate itself. That's how it felt, anyway.

JEFF. How does it feel now?

SERENA. The longing's still a part of me. But if I have to have that longing, that ache... maybe I have to learn to use it better.

JEFF. Can we learn together?

SERENA. I think so. Yeah.

JEFF *puts his arm around her. She leans against him.* MILES *sings and plays while*

BRIDGET *listens.*

MILES. When we were children things were so easy
    The rules of our lives were writ clear
    A wife or a husband, a house and a mortgage
    Some kids just to prove we were here

    Then as we got older we made ourselves bankrupt
    Searching too hard for 'the one'
    Love was a broker who sold us false promises
    Investments without a return

    But love doesn't come in a limousine
    It's happy to wait for the bus
    As long as there's you and there's me
    There's always an 'us'

    A couple of square pegs chafing our edges
    Trying to fit into the holes
    Thinking that we'd failed our Human Certificate
    When all along we had struck gold

    Cos love doesn't always make flesh and blood
    Or come in a unit of three
    As long as there's you and there's I
    There's always a 'we'

    Now we are wiser
    Two wooden soldiers
    Half of the way through our lives
    The nuclear family was just propaganda
    And the scales fell away from our eyes

    So I'll be your nephew and you can be auntie
    The kind who knows how to have fun
    I'll be your big sister if you'll be my father
    And sometimes a firm-but-fair mum

    Cos families aren't made in laboratories
    Or forged in the heavens above
    As long as there's you
    As long as there's me
    There'll always be love

    As long as there's you and there's me
    There'll always be love

*A school bell rings. The kids' chatter fades out as they go
back inside.*

End.

MUSIC

The Bag Song (Part 1)

words by Jemma Kennedy
music by Zara Nunn

The Bag Song (Part 1) | Genesis Inc.

The Bag Song (Part 1) | Genesis Inc.

The Bag Song (Part 2)

words by Jemma Kennedy
music by Zara Nunn

The Bag Song (Part 2) | Genesis Inc.

no more blind dates and birth con-trol pills.......... Now she's

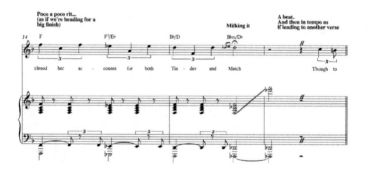

Poco a poco rit...
(as if we're heading for a big finish)

Milking it

A beat.
And then in tempo as if leading to another verse

closed her ac - counts for both Tin - der and Match Though to

keep up mo-rale she still wax - es her -

The Song of Us

words by Jemma Kennedy
music by Zara Nunn

The Song of Us | Genesis Inc.

The Song of Us ! Genesis Inc.

A little fuller wth a touch more pace

The Song of Us | Genesis Inc.

The Song of Us | Genesis Inc.

The Song of Us | Genesis Inc.